Hymns for the Revised Common Lectionary

2009

Hymns for the Revised Common Lectionary 2009

Year B

Dean B. McIntyre

DISCIPLESHIP RESOURCES

P O BOX 340003 • NASHVILLE, TN 37203-0003
www.discipleshipresources.org

ISBN 978-0-88177-547-1
Library of Congress Control Number 2008935370

Introduction

One of the great benefits of using the Revised Common Lectionary (RCL) in preaching and planning worship is that it engages the congregation in the entirety of Scripture. The broad scope of the Bible's contents is systematically unfolded by preachers and planners who use the RCL, exposing the people to more than a selection of favorite Scriptures, stories, concepts, and topical issues.

It is the same with selecting hymns and songs for the congregation to sing: how often are we tempted to sing the same selections over and over again? Every congregation develops its own body of favorites, which is sometimes quite small. Worship planners who use *Hymns for the Revised Common Lectionary* have available lists of hymns and songs related to every RCL reading for the entire year. Using the lists each week will allow planners to expand beyond the small list of favorites and use much more of the hymnal's contents, thus enriching a congregation's worship and singing experience.

Hymns for the Revised Common Lectionary offers suggestions for hymns related to every Old Testament, Psalm, Epistle, and New Testament reading for every Sunday and major observance of the liturgical year. Use it together with the Topical Index found in the back of most hymnals. Worship planners of all denominations will find this volume useful. *Hymns for the Revised Common Lectionary* includes recommended hymns for six specific hymnals and songbooks:

UMH   *The United Methodist Hymnal* (Nashville: The United Methodist Publishing House, 1989)

MVPC   *Mil Voces Para Celebrar: Himnario Metodista* (Nashville: The United Methodist Publishing House, 1996)

CLUW   *Come, Let Us Worship: The Korean-English United Methodist Hymnal; Book of United Methodist Worship* (Nashville: The United Methodist Publishing House, 2001)

TFWS   *The Faith We Sing* (Nashville: Abingdon Press, 2000)

SOZ   *Songs of Zion* (Nashville: Abingdon Press, 1981)

URW   *Upper Room Worshipbook: Music and Liturgies for Spiritual Formation* (Nashville: Upper Room Books, 2006)

Also included is a helpful monthly planning calendar that includes: lectionary reading citations for every Sunday and major observance, major feast days and celebrations of the liturgical year, and major holidays and observances of the civil calendar.

Dean B. McIntyre
Director of Music Resources, The Center for Worship Resourcing
The General Board of Discipleship of The United Methodist Church

November 30, 2008 (First Sunday of Advent)

Liturgical Color: Purple or Blue

Scripture Hymn Title	UMH	MVPC	CLUW	TFWS	SOZ	URW
Isaiah 64:1-9						
All My Hope Is Firmly Grounded	132					
As a Fire Is Meant for Burning				2237		
Change My Heart, O God			278	2152		
Have Thine Own Way, Lord!	382	213	327			
How Like a Gentle Spirit	115		216			
Jesus, Lover of My Soul	479					
O Come and Dwell in Me	388					
O Thou, in Whose Presence My Soul Takes Delight	518					
Open Our Eyes				2086		
Water, River, Spirit, Grace				2253		
Psalm 80:1-7, 17-19						
Come, Thou Long-Expected Jesus	196	82				101
Creator of the Earth and Skies	450					
God of Grace and God of Glory	577	287				
Great Is Thy Faithfulness	140	30	81			
I Want to Walk as a Child of the Light	206		102			
Lead Me, Guide Me				2214		
Lift Up Your Heads, Ye Mighty Gates	213					
Lord, Listen to Your Children				2207		
Nothing between My Soul and My Savior	373				21	
O Come, O Come, Emmanuel	211	80				
O Day of God, Draw Nigh	730					
O God in Heaven, Grant to Thy Children	119		227			
O God of Every Nation	435					
O God Who Shaped Creation	443					
Out of the Depths				2136		
People, Look East	202					

7

Scripture Hymn Title	UMH	MVPC	CLUW	TFWS	SOZ	URW
Send Your Word	195		113			
Shepherd Me, O God				2058		
Shine, Jesus, Shine			264	2173		
The First Song of Isaiah				2030		
Unsettled World				2183		
Wake, Awake, for Night Is Flying	720					
We Are Called				2172		
Wellspring of Wisdom	506					173
Wounded World that Cries for Healing				2177		

1 Corinthians 1:3-9

	UMH	MVPC	CLUW	TFWS	SOZ	URW
Blessed Be the God of Israel	209					12
Come, Holy Ghost, Our Souls Inspire	651					
Great Is Thy Faithfulness	140	30	81			
I Know Whom I Have Believed (I Know Not Why God's Wondrous Grace)	714		290			
Nothing between My Soul and My Savior	373				21	
Send Your Word	195		113			
To God Be the Glory, Great Things He Hath Done!	98	169	78			

Mark 13:24-37

	UMH	MVPC	CLUW	TFWS	SOZ	URW
Come, Thou Long-Expected Jesus	196	82				101
Freedom Is Coming				2192		
I Know Whom I Have Believed (I Know Not Why God's Wondrous Grace)	714		290			
Joy Comes with the Dawn				2210		
Let All Mortal Flesh Keep Silence	626		150		217	
Lo, He Comes with Clouds Descending	718					
My Lord, What a Morning	719		386		145	
O Day of God, Draw Nigh	730					
O Freedom				2194		
O Mary, Don't You Weep, Don't You Mourn	134				153	
People, Look East	202					
Sing with All the Saints in Glory	702		382			
Soon and Very Soon	706		385		198	
There's Something About that Name	171	74				
Wake, Awake, for Night Is Flying	720					
When We All Get to Heaven (Sing the Wondrous Love of Jesus)	701	383	381		15	

December 7, 2008 (Second Sunday of Advent)
Liturgical Color: Purple or Blue

Scripture Hymn Title	UMH	MVPC	CLUW	TFWS	SOZ	URW
Isaiah 40:1-11						
All Earth Is Waiting to See the Promised One (Toda la Tierra Espera al Salvador)	210	78				
Alleluia	186		355			
Blessed Be the God of Israel	209					12
Blessed Quietness				2142	206	
Canticle of Mary	199					
Go, Tell It on the Mountain	251	97			75	
Great Is the Lord				2022		
Hail to the Lord's Anointed	203	81				
Heralds of Christ, Who Bear the King's Commands	567					
Here at Jordan's River						106
How Firm a Foundation	529	256				
I Love You, Lord				2068		
In the Lord I'll Be Ever Thankful				2195		381
Lord God, Almighty				2006		
O Lord, Your Tenderness				2143		
On Jordan's Stormy Banks I Stand	724				54	
Prepare the Way of the Lord	207		141			
Savior, Like a Shepherd Lead Us	381					
Wake, Awake, for Night Is Flying	720					
Psalm 85:1-2, 8-13						
Lift Up Your Heads, Ye Mighty Gates	213					
O Come, O Come, Emmanuel	211	80				
O God in Heaven, Grant to Thy Children	119		227			
O God, Our Help in Ages Past	117					200
Send Your Word	195		113			

Scripture Hymn Title	UMH	MVPC	CLUW	TFWS	SOZ	URW
2 Peter 3:8-15a						
Forth in Thy Name, O Lord, I Go	438					
Freedom Is Coming				2192		
I Want to Be Ready	722				151	
Not So in Haste, My Heart	455					
O Day of God, Draw Nigh	730					
O God, Our Help in Ages Past	117					200
Shalom to You (Somos Del Señor)	666		361			
This Is a Day of New Beginnings	383	208	311			
Mark 1:1-8						
A Charge to Keep I Have	413					
Alleluia	186		355			
Angels from the Realms of Glory	220					
Blessed Be the God of Israel	209					12
Come, Ye Sinners, Poor and Needy	340					
Depth of Mercy! Can There Be	355		273			
Heralds of Christ, Who Bear the King's Commands	567					
Jesus, Name above All Names				2071		
O Come, O Come, Emmanuel	211	80				
On Jordan's Stormy Banks I Stand	724				54	
Prepare the Way of the Lord	207		141			
There's Something About that Name	171	74				
'Tis the Old Ship of Zion	345				131	
Wild and Lone the Prophet's Voice				2089		

December 14, 2008 (Third Sunday of Advent)

Liturgical Color: Purple or Blue

Scripture Hymn Title	UMH	MVPC	CLUW	TFWS	SOZ	URW
Isaiah 61:1-4, 8-11						
Arise, Your Light Is Come						138
Break Thou the Bread of Life	599					
Come, All of You	350					
Come, Thou Long-Expected Jesus	196	82				101
Hail to the Lord's Anointed	203	81				
Hark! the Herald Angels Sing	240	101				
Holy God, We Praise Thy Name	79		80			
Holy, Holy				2039		
Holy, Holy, Holy! Lord God Almighty	64	4	79			
Hosanna! Hosanna!				2109		
Jesus Shall Reign Where'er the Sun	157					
Jesus! the Name High over All	193		199			
Mil Voces Para Celebrar	59					
Morning Glory, Starlit Sky	194					
O For a Thousand Tongues to Sing	57	1	226			
O Lord, Your Tenderness				2143		
O Zion, Haste	573					
On Jordan's Stormy Banks I Stand	724				54	
Praise, My Soul, the King of Heaven	66					75
Santo! ¡Santo! ¡Santo!	65					
Tell Out, My Soul, the Greatness of the Lord!	200					
The Spirit Sends Us Forth to Serve				2241		
The Summons				2130		60
We Are Called				2172		
Wounded World that Cries for Healing				2177		

Scripture Hymn Title	UMH	MVPC	CLUW	TFWS	SOZ	URW
Psalm 126						
Bless His Holy Name				2015		
Come, Ye Disconsolate, Where'er Ye Languish	510					
Give to the Winds Thy Fears	129		282			
God Has Done Great Things for Us (Psalm 126)						326
Hail to the Lord's Anointed	203	81				
Joy Comes with the Dawn				2210		
Let's Sing Unto the Lord (Cantemos al Señor)	149	49	67			
O God, Our Help in Ages Past	117					200
O Spirit of the Living God	539					
Rejoice, Ye Pure in Heart (MARION)	160		130			
Rejoice, Ye Pure in Heart (VINEYARD HAVEN)	161					
When God First Brought Us Back from Exile (Psalm 126)						325
When God Restored Our Common Life				2182		
1 Thessalonians 5:16-24						
Every Time I Feel the Spirit	404		213		121	
Give Thanks			247	2036		
God Be with You till We Meet Again (GOD BE WITH YOU)	672		347		37	
God Be with You till We Meet Again (RANDOLPH)	673					
He Who Began a Good Work in You				2163		
I'm Goin'a Sing When the Spirit Says Sing	333		223		81	
Jesus, We Are Here				2273		
Lord, Listen to Your Children Praying				2193		
Prayer Is the Soul's Sincere Desire	492					
Rejoice, Ye Pure in Heart (MARION)	160		130			
Rejoice, Ye Pure in Heart (VINEYARD HAVEN)	161					
Take Time to Be Holy	395					
The Fragrance of Christ				2205		
Thou Hidden Love of God	414					
What a Friend We Have in Jesus	526	257	333			

Scripture Hymn Title	UMH	MVPC	CLUW	TFWS	SOZ	URW

John 1:6-8, 19-28

Scripture Hymn Title	UMH	MVPC	CLUW	TFWS	SOZ	URW
Christ Is the World's Light	188					
Give Me the Faith Which Can Remove	650					
God Hath Spoken by the Prophets	108	38				
Hark! the Herald Angels Sing	240	101				
Heralds of Christ, Who Bear the King's Commands	567					
I Want to Walk as a Child of the Light	206		102			
Jesus, Name above All Names				2071		
Savior of the Nations, Come	214					
Send Your Word	195		113			
This Is the Spirit's Entry Now	608					
Wild and Lone the Prophet's Voice				2089		
Word of God, Come Down on Earth	182					

December 21, 2008 (Fourth Sunday of Advent)

Liturgical Color: Purple or Blue

Scripture Hymn Title	UMH	MVPC	CLUW	TFWS	SOZ	URW
2 Samuel 7:1-11, 16						
Blessed Be the God of Israel	209					12
God Will Take Care of You (Nunca desmayes)	130	260				
Hail to the Lord's Anointed	203	81				
It Came upon the Midnight Clear	218	90				
Jesus Shall Reign Where'er the Sun	157					
O Come, O Come, Emmanuel	211	80				
That Boy-Child of Mary	241					
Luke 1:47-55						
Arise, Shine				2005		
Bless His Holy Name				2015		
Blessed Be the God of Israel	209					12
Blest Are They				2155		163
Canticle of Mary	199					
Canticle of the Turning						18
Freedom Is Coming				2192		
Gather Us In				2236		54
Give Thanks			247	2036		
Glory to God				2033		
God Is So Good				2056	231	
Hail to the Lord's Anointed	203	81				
He Is Born, the Holy Child	228	117	156			
Holy Ground				2272		
Holy Is Your Name						20
I'm So Glad Jesus Lifted Me				2151		
In the Bleak Midwinter	221					

Scripture	Hymn Title	UMH	MVPC	CLUW	TFWS	SOZ	URW
	It Came upon the Midnight Clear	218	90				
	Joseph Dearest, Joseph Mine				2099		
	Joy to the World, the Lord Is Come!	246	100	161			
	Lo, How a Rose E'er Blooming	216					
	My Soul Gives Glory to My God	198					
	My Soul Proclaims the Greatness of the Lord						17
	My Soul Proclaims with Wonder						19
	O Come, All Ye Faithful	234	106				
	O Come, O Come, Emmanuel	211	80				
	Once in Royal David's City	250		159			
	People, Look East	202					
	Praise to the Lord				2029		309
	Savior of the Nations, Come	214					
	She Comes Sailing on the Wind				2122		
	Sing for God's Glory						62
	Sing of Mary, Pure and Lowly	272					
	Tell Out, My Soul, the Greatness of the Lord!	200					
	That Boy-Child of Mary	241					
	The First One Ever, Oh, Ever to Know	276					
	The First Song of Isaiah				2030		
	The Snow Lay on the Ground			163	2093		
	The Virgin Mary Had a Baby Boy				2098		
	To a Maid Engaged to Joseph	215		151			
	What Does the Lord Require	441					
	What Does the Lord Require of You				2174		
	When the Poor Ones (Cuando El Pobre)	434	301	138			
	Ye Who Claim the Faith of Jesus	197					

Romans 16:25-27

Scripture	Hymn Title	UMH	MVPC	CLUW	TFWS	SOZ	URW
	All Earth Is Waiting to See the Promised One (Toda la Tierra Espera al Salvador)	210	78				
	Come, Holy Ghost, Our Hearts Inspire	603		218			
	Let All the World in Every Corner Sing	93					
	To God Be the Glory, Great Things He Hath Done!	98	169	78			

Luke 1:26-38

Scripture	Hymn Title	UMH	MVPC	CLUW	TFWS	SOZ	URW
	All Earth Is Waiting to See the Promised One (Toda la Tierra Espera al Salvador)	210	78				

Scripture Hymn Title	UMH	MVPC	CLUW	TFWS	SOZ	URW
At the Name of Jesus Every Knee Shall Bow	168					
Blest Are They				2155		163
Creator of the Stars of Night	692					218
He Is Born, the Holy Child	228	117	156			
I'm So Glad Jesus Lifted Me				2151		
In the Bleak Midwinter	221					
Jesus, Name above All Names				2071		
Joseph Dearest, Joseph Mine				2099		
Lo, How a Rose E'er Blooming	216					
Make Me a Servant				2176		
My Soul Gives Glory to My God	198					
O Come, All Ye Faithful	234	106				
Of the Father's Love Begotten	184	52	66			
Once in Royal David's City	250		159			
People, Look East	202					
Savior of the Nations, Come	214					
She Comes Sailing on the Wind				2122		
Sing of Mary, Pure and Lowly	272					
Tell Out, My Soul, the Greatness of the Lord!	200					
That Boy-Child of Mary	241					
The First One Ever, Oh, Ever to Know	276					
The Snow Lay on the Ground			163	2093		
The Virgin Mary Had a Baby Boy				2098		
There's Something About that Name	171	74				
To a Maid Engaged to Joseph	215		151			
Ye Who Claim the Faith of Jesus	197					

December 24, 2008 (Christmas Eve)

Liturgical Color: White or Gold

Scripture Hymn Title	UMH	MVPC	CLUW	TFWS	SOZ	URW
Isaiah 9:2-7						
All Earth Is Waiting to See the Promised One (Toda la Tierra Espera al Salvador)	210	78				
Arise, Shine Out, Your Light Has Come	725					
Break Forth, O Beauteous Heavenly Light	223					
Canticle of Light and Darkness	205					
Christ, Whose Glory Fills the Skies	173		281			
Come Now, O Prince of Peace (O-so-so)			148	2232		415
Come, Thou Long-Expected Jesus	196	82				101
Gather Us In				2236		54
Goodness Is Stronger than Evil				2219		436
Hark! the Herald Angels Sing	240	101				
His Name Is Wonderful	174	172	203			
How Majestic Is Your Name				2023		
I Want to Walk as a Child of the Light	206		102			
It Came upon the Midnight Clear	218	90				
Jesus, Name above All Names				2071		
King of Kings				2075		
Light of the World				2204		
O Come, All Ye Faithful	234	106				
O Day of Peace that Dimly Shines	729					
O Morning Star, How Fair and Bright	247					
O Splendor of God's Glory Bright	679					211
Shine, Jesus, Shine			264	2173		
The God of Abraham Praise	116	28				
We Are Called				2172		
We've a Story to Tell to the Nations	569					
What a Mighty God We Serve				2021		

17

Scripture Hymn Title	UMH	MVPC	CLUW	TFWS	SOZ	URW
Psalm 96						
Amen, We Praise Your Name, O God (Amen Siakudumisa)				2067		398
Canticle of Praise to God	91					
Great Is the Lord				2022		
Hark! the Herald Angels Sing	240	101				
Holy God, We Praise Thy Name	79		80			
Honor and Praise				2018		
How Great Thou Art	77	2	61			
I Sing Praises to Your Name				2037		
In the Bleak Midwinter	221					
King of Kings				2075		
Majesty, Worship His Majesty	176	171	204			
Mil Voces Para Celebrar	59					
O For a Thousand Tongues to Sing	57	1	226			
Of the Father's Love Begotten	184	52	66			
On This Day Earth Shall Ring	248					
Praise the Lord Who Reigns Above	96		124			
Praise, My Soul, the King of Heaven	66					75
Praise, Praise, Praise the Lord				2035		399
Shout to the Lord				2074		
Sing a New Song to the Lord				2045		
Sing Alleluia to the Lord				2258		404
Sing We Now of Christmas	237		166			
Someone Asked the Question				2144		
We Sing of Your Glory				2011		
We Sing to You, O God				2001		293
Titus 2:11-14						
A Charge to Keep I Have	413					
Blessed Assurance, Jesus Is Mine!	369	65	287			
Break Forth, O Beauteous Heavenly Light	223					
Come, Thou Long-Expected Jesus	196	82				101
Good Christian Friends, Rejoice	224		155			
Here Is Bread, Here Is Wine				2266		
I Love You, Lord				2068		
I Need Thee Every Hour	397					
I Want a Principle Within	410					

Scripture	Hymn Title	UMH	MVPC	CLUW	TFWS	SOZ	URW
	In the Singing				2255		
	Joy to the World, the Lord Is Come!	246	100	161			
	Lord, I Lift Your Name on High				2088		
	My Hope Is Built on Nothing Less	368	261				
	O Master, Let Me Walk with Thee	430		315			
	On This Day Earth Shall Ring	248					
	Rise Up, Shepherd, and Follow				2096		
	Sing Alleluia to the Lord				2258		404

Luke 2:1-20

Scripture	Hymn Title	UMH	MVPC	CLUW	TFWS	SOZ	URW
	Amen, Amen				2072		
	Angels from the Realms of Glory	220					
	Angels We Have Heard on High	238	98				
	At the Name of Jesus Every Knee Shall Bow	168					
	Away in a Manger	217	93	157			
	Break Forth, O Beauteous Heavenly Light	223					
	Canticle of God's Glory	83					
	Child So Lovely, Here I Kneel Before You (Niño Lindo, Ante Ti Me Rindo)	222	114				
	Come and See				2127		
	Dona Nobis Pacem	376	360	142			443
	Gloria, Gloria	72		353			380
	Glory Be to the Father (GREATOREX)	71					
	Glory to God				2033		
	Glory to God in the Highest				2276		
	Go, Tell It on the Mountain	251	97			75	
	Good Christian Friends, Rejoice	224		155			
	Hark! the Herald Angels Sing	240	101				
	He Came Down				2085		
	Holy God, We Praise Thy Name	79		80			
	I Sing Praises to Your Name				2037		
	In the Bleak Midwinter	221					
	Infant Holy, Infant Lowly	229	116	152			
	It Came upon the Midnight Clear	218	90				
	Jesus, Our Brother, Strong and Good	227					
	Joseph Dearest, Joseph Mine				2099		
	Joy to the World, the Lord Is Come!	246	100	161			
	Jubilate, Servite				2017		383

Scripture Hymn Title	UMH	MVPC	CLUW	TFWS	SOZ	URW
Lift High the Cross	159	164	174			
Like a Child				2092		
Lo, How a Rose E'er Blooming	216					
Lord, I Lift Your Name on High				2088		
Maker, in Whom We Live	88					
O Come, All Ye Faithful	234	106				
O Day of Peace that Dimly Shines	729					
O Sing a Song of Bethlehem	179					
Of the Father's Love Begotten	184	52	66			
On This Day Earth Shall Ring	248					
Once in Royal David's City	250		159			
One Holy Night in Bethlehem				2097		
Rise Up, Shepherd, and Follow				2096		
Savior of the Nations, Come	214					
Silent Night, Holy Night	239	103	160			
Sing We Now of Christmas	237		166			
Spirit, Spirit of Gentleness				2120		
Star-Child				2095		
That Boy-Child of Mary	241					
The First Noel the Angel Did Say	245	89				
The Friendly Beasts	227					
The Snow Lay on the Ground			163	2093		
The Virgin Mary Had a Baby Boy				2098		
There's a Song in the Air	249					
Thou Didst Leave Thy Throne			172	2100		
'Twas in the Moon of Wintertime	244					
We Sing of Your Glory				2011		
What Child Is This	219	112	154			
When Christmas Morn Is Dawning	232					
While Shepherds Watched Their Flocks by Night	236					
Woman in the Night	274					

December 25, 2008 (Christmas Day)

Liturgical Color: White

Scripture Hymn Title	UMH	MVPC	CLUW	TFWS	SOZ	URW
Isaiah 52:7-10						
Come, Thou Long-Expected Jesus	196	82				101
Good Christian Friends, Rejoice	224		155			
Joy to the World, the Lord Is Come!	246	100	161			
Let Us with a Joyful Mind				2012		
Prepare the Way of the Lord	207		141			
Someone Asked the Question				2144		
Wake, Awake, for Night Is Flying	720					
Psalm 98						
All Creatures of Our God and King	62	22				
Camina, Pueblo de Dios (Walk On, O People of God)	305	151				
Children of the Heavenly Father	141		335			
Clap Your Hands				2028		
Joy to the World, the Lord Is Come!	246	100	161			
Let All the World in Every Corner Sing	93					
Let's Sing Unto the Lord (Cantemos al Señor)	149	49	67			
Praise the Lord Who Reigns Above	96		124			
Praise the Lord with the Sound of Trumpet				2020		
Praise to the Lord, the Almighty	139	29	68			63
Shout to the Lord				2074		
Sing a New Song (Psalm 98)						296
Sing a New Song to the Lord				2045		
The Head that Once Was Crowned with Thorns	326					
The Strife Is O'er, the Battle Done	306					
The Trees of the Field				2279		
When in Our Music God Is Glorified	68		129			

21

Scripture Hymn Title	UMH	MVPC	CLUW	TFWS	SOZ	URW

Hebrews 1:1-4 (5-12)

Scripture Hymn Title	UMH	MVPC	CLUW	TFWS	SOZ	URW
Angels We Have Heard on High	238	98				
God Hath Spoken by the Prophets	108	38				
Holy God, We Praise Thy Name	79		80			
Infant Holy, Infant Lowly	229	116	152			
O Come, All Ye Faithful	234	106				
Of the Father's Love Begotten	184	52	66			
Rejoice, the Lord Is King (DARWALL'S 148TH)	715					
Rejoice, the Lord Is King (GOPSAL)	716					
The Day Thou Gavest, Lord, Is Ended	690					
The Head that Once Was Crowned with Thorns	326					
Thou Art Worthy				2041		
Ye Servants of God, Your Master Proclaim	181					

John 1:1-14

Scripture Hymn Title	UMH	MVPC	CLUW	TFWS	SOZ	URW
At the Name of Jesus Every Knee Shall Bow	168					
Break Forth, O Beauteous Heavenly Light	223					
Christ Is the World's Light	188					
Christ the Eternal Lord						94
Christ the Lord Is Risen				2116		
Christ, Whose Glory Fills the Skies	173		281			
Cold December Flies Away	233					
Come, Thou Almighty King	61	11				
En el Frío Invernal	233					
Go, Tell It on the Mountain	251	97			75	
Good Christian Friends, Rejoice	224		155			
Hail, Thou Once Despised Jesus	325					
Hark! the Herald Angels Sing	240	101				
I Want to Walk as a Child of the Light	206		102			
I Was There to Hear Your Borning Cry				2051		
Jesus, Joy of Our Desiring	644		344			
Jesus, Name above All Names				2071		
Joy to the World, the Lord Is Come!	246	100	161			
Light of the World				2204		
Lord, I Lift Your Name on High				2088		
Love Came Down at Christmas	242					
Morning Has Broken	145	354	370			186

Scripture Hymn Title	UMH	MVPC	CLUW	TFWS	SOZ	URW
Mothering God, You Gave Me Birth				2050		
Now It Is Evening				2187		
Now, on Land and Sea Descending	685		372			
O Come, All Ye Faithful	234	106				
O Holy Spirit, Root of Life				2121		79
O Love that Wilt Not Let Me Go	480	255	322			
O Morning Star, How Fair and Bright	247					
O Word of God Incarnate	598					
Of the Father's Love Begotten	184	52	66			
On This Day Earth Shall Ring	248					
Send Your Word	195		113			
Shine, Jesus, Shine			264	2173		
Sing of Mary, Pure and Lowly	272					
Thou Art Worthy				2041		
Thou Didst Leave Thy Throne			172	2100		
We Are Singing\We Are Marching\Siyahamba				2235		
When Christmas Morn Is Dawning	232					
Womb of Life				2046		
Word of God, Come Down on Earth	182					

December 28, 2008 (First Sunday after Christmas Day)

Liturgical Color: White or Gold

Scripture Hymn Title	UMH	MVPC	CLUW	TFWS	SOZ	URW
Isaiah 61:10–62:3						
All Hail the Power of Jesus' Name (CORONATION)	154	60				
All Hail the Power of Jesus' Name (DIADEM)	155					
Break Forth, O Beauteous Heavenly Light	223					
Come, Thou Almighty King	61	11				
Deck Thyself, My Soul, with Gladness	612					
Hark! the Herald Angels Sing	240	101				
Here, O My Lord, I See Thee	623					
Joy to the World, the Lord Is Come!	246	100	161			
Lo, How a Rose E'er Blooming	216					
Psalm 148						
All Creatures of Our God and King	62	22				
All You Works of God, Bless the Lord!						97
Clap Your Hands				2028		
Creation Sings! Each Plant and Tree						86
Glory to God				2033		
God of the Sparrow God of the Whale	122	37	59			
Good Christian Friends, Rejoice	224		155			
Great God, Your Love Has Called Us Here						87
Great Is the Lord				2022		
Halle, Halle, Halleluja				2026		370
How Great Thou Art	77	2	61			
I Love to Tell the Story	156	56				
I Sing the Almighty Power of God	152		65			
I Want to Praise Your Name (Psalms 148-150)						364

Scripture	Hymn Title	UMH	MVPC	CLUW	TFWS	SOZ	URW
	Joyful, Joyful, We Adore Thee	89	5	75			65
	Jubilate, Servite				2017		383
	Let All Things Now Living				2008		
	Let Us with a Joyful Mind				2012		
	Praise the Lord Who Reigns Above	96		124			
	Praise the Lord with the Sound of Trumpet				2020		
	Praise to the Lord, the Almighty	139	29	68			63
	Praise, Praise, Praise the Lord				2035		399
	Sing a New Song to the Lord				2045		
	Sing Praise to God Who Reigns Above	126		60			70
	Sing the Lord a New Song (Psalm 148)						365
	The Trees of the Field				2279		
	We Will Glorify the King of Kings				2087		
	What a Mighty God We Serve				2021		
	Ye Watchers and Ye Holy Ones	90					

Galatians 4:4-7

Scripture	Hymn Title	UMH	MVPC	CLUW	TFWS	SOZ	URW
	Children of the Heavenly Father	141		335			
	Hark! the Herald Angels Sing	240	101				
	O God in Heaven, Grant to Thy Children	119		227			
	Once in Royal David's City	250		159			
	That Boy-Child of Mary	241					
	'Twas in the Moon of Wintertime	244					

Luke 2:22-40

Scripture	Hymn Title	UMH	MVPC	CLUW	TFWS	SOZ	URW
	A Mother Lined a Basket				2189		
	All Earth Is Waiting to See the Promised One (Toda la Tierra Espera al Salvador)	210	78				
	Angels from the Realms of Glory	220					
	At the Name of Jesus Every Knee Shall Bow	168					
	Away in a Manger	217	93	157			
	Canticle of Simeon	225					
	Child So Lovely, Here I Kneel Before You (Niño Lindo, Ante Ti Me Rindo)	222	114				
	Come, Thou Long-Expected Jesus	196	82				101
	Go Now in Peace	665		363			
	He Is Born, the Holy Child	228	117	156			
	Jesus, Name above All Names				2071		
	Joy to the World, the Lord Is Come!	246	100	161			

Scripture Hymn Title	UMH	MVPC	CLUW	TFWS	SOZ	URW
Let Us Now Depart in Thy Peace	668					
Let Your Servant Now Go in Peace						385
Like a Child				2092		
Lord, Dismiss Us with Thy Blessing	671					
Lord, Let Your Servant						25
My Master, See, the Time Has Come	226					
Now Let Your Servant Go						27
Now, Lord, You Have Kept Your Word						26
Our Parent, by Whose Name	447					
Rock-a-Bye, My Dear Little Boy	235					
She Comes Sailing on the Wind				2122		
Sing We Now of Christmas	237	166				
Song of Simeon						24
That Boy-Child of Mary	241					
There's a Song in the Air	249					

December 31, 2008 (Watch Night)

Liturgical Color: White

Scripture Hymn Title	UMH	MVPC	CLUW	TFWS	SOZ	URW
Ecclesiastes 3:1-13						
All Things Bright and Beautiful	147		63			
Beams of Heaven as I Go	524				10	
By Gracious Powers So Wonderfully Sheltered	517					
For One Great Peace				2185		
For the Fruits of This Creation	97					193
Forth in Thy Name, O Lord, I Go	438					
From the Rising of the Sun				2024		
God of the Ages	698	377				
Great Is Thy Faithfulness	140	30	81			
Hymn of Promise (In the Bulb There Is a Flower)	707	338	392			
I Was There to Hear Your Borning Cry				2051		
In His Time				2203		
O God, Our Help in Ages Past	117					200
Psalm 8						
All Creatures of Our God and King	62	22				
Amen, We Praise Your Name, O God (Amen Siakudumisa)				2067		398
Awesome God				2040		
Children of the Heavenly Father	141		335			
Creator of the Earth and Skies						450
For the Beauty of the Earth	92	8				
For the Fruits of This Creation	97					193
From the Rising of the Sun				2024		
Glory to God in the Highest				2276		
God Created Heaven and Earth	151					

Scripture Hymn Title	UMH	MVPC	CLUW	TFWS	SOZ	URW
God, Our God, Your Glorious Name (Psalm 8)						229
God, Whose Love Is Reigning o'er Us	100		73			74
Great Is the Lord				2022		
How Great Thou Art	77	2	61			
How Majestic Is Your Name				2023		
I Sing the Almighty Power of God	152		65			
Joyful, Joyful, We Adore Thee	89	5	75			65
Many and Great, O God, Are Thy Things	148	50	71			232
O God Beyond All Praising				2009		
O God in Heaven, Grant to Thy Children	119		227			
O God, Our Help in Ages Past	117					200
O Lord, Our Lord (Psalm 8)						231
Praise, My Soul, the King of Heaven	66					75
Prayer Is the Soul's Sincere Desire	492					

Revelation 21:1-6a

Scripture Hymn Title	UMH	MVPC	CLUW	TFWS	SOZ	URW
All Who Hunger				2126		
Arise, Shine Out, Your Light Has Come	725					
Awesome God				2040		
Beams of Heaven as I Go	524				10	
Blessed Quietness				2142	206	
Christ the Victorious, Give to Your Servants	653		380			
Come, Let Us Join Our Friends Above	709		387			
Come, We that Love the Lord (Marching to Zion)	733				3	139
Come, Ye Disconsolate, Where'er Ye Languish		510				
For All the Saints				2283		
For the Healing of the Nations	428					
From the Rising of the Sun				2024		
Glorious Things of Thee Are Spoken	731		256			
Here, O My Lord, I See Thee	623					
I Want to Be Ready	722				151	
I'll Fly Away				2282	183	
Joy Comes with the Dawn				2210		
Joy in the Morning				2284		
Love Divine, All Loves Excelling	384					100
My Faith Looks Up to Thee	452				215	

Scripture Hymn Title	UMH	MVPC	CLUW	TFWS	SOZ	URW
O Come and Dwell in Me	388					
O Day of Peace that Dimly Shines	729					
O Freedom				2194		
O God, Our Help in Ages Past	117					200
O Holy City, Seen of John	726		390			
O What Their Joy and Their Glory Must Be	727					
Open Our Eyes				2086		
Sing with All the Saints in Glory	702		382			
Soon and Very Soon	706		385		198	
Spirit Song	347	190	91			
There's a Spirit in the Air	192					
There's Something About that Name	171	74				
There's Within My Heart a Melody	380		289			
This Is a Day of New Beginnings	383	208	311			
This Is the Feast of Victory	638					
We Shall Overcome	533		140		127	
We Will Glorify the King of Kings				2087		
When All Is Ended						133
You Who Are Thirsty				2132		

Matthew 25:31-46

Scripture Hymn Title	UMH	MVPC	CLUW	TFWS	SOZ	URW
All Who Hunger				2126		
All Who Love and Serve Your City	433					
As We Gather at Your Table				2268		
Carol of the Epiphany				2094		
Christ Is the World's Light	188					
Come, Share the Lord				2269		
Come, Sinners, to the Gospel Feast _Communion_	616					
Come, Ye Disconsolate, Where'er Ye Languish	510					
Come, Ye Thankful People, Come	694		241			
Crown Him with Many Crowns	327	157				
For One Great Peace				2185		
For the Healing of the Nations	428					
Forward Through the Ages	555					
Gather Us In				2236		54
God Weeps				2048		

Scripture Hymn Title	UMH	MVPC	CLUW	TFWS	SOZ	URW
Here Am I				2178		
How Can We Name a Love	111					
I Come with Joy to Meet My Lord	617					120
In Remembrance of Me				2254		
Jesu, Jesu, Fill Us with Your Love	432	288	179			116
Jesus' Hands Were Kind Hands	273		176			
Lord, Whose Love Through Humble Service	581					204
Now It Is Evening				2187		
O God, Our Help in Ages Past	117					200
People Need the Lord				2244		
Rescue the Perishing	591					
Shout to the Lord				2074		
Star-Child				2095		
Sunday's Palms Are Wednesday's Ashes				2138		
There's a Spirit in the Air	192					
Together We Serve				2175		
We Gather Together to Ask the Lord's Blessing	131	361				
What Does the Lord Require of You				2174		
When the Church of Jesus Shuts Its Outer Door	592					
When the Poor Ones (Cuando El Pobre)	434	301	138			
Where Cross the Crowded Ways of Life	427	296				
Wounded World that Cries for Healing				2177		

January 4, 2009 (Second Sunday after Christmas) (May also celebrate Epiphany of the Lord using Scriptures for January 6)

Liturgical Color: White

Scripture Hymn Title	UMH	MVPC	CLUW	TFWS	SOZ	URW
Jeremiah 31:7-14						
Alleluia	186		355			
Break Forth, O Beauteous Heavenly Light	223					
Come Back Quickly to the Lord	343		272			
Depth of Mercy! Can There Be	355		273			
From All that Dwell Below the Skies	101		126			
Gather Us In				2236		54
I'll Praise My Maker While I've Breath	60		123			
Let All the World in Every Corner Sing	93					
Lift Every Voice and Sing	519				32	
Marvelous Grace of Our Loving Lord	365					
Praise, My Soul, the King of Heaven	66					75
Seek the Lord Who Now Is Present	124					
Sing a New Song to the Lord				2045		
Someone Asked the Question				2144		
Stand Up and Bless the Lord	662		128			
There's a Wideness in God's Mercy	121					
Psalm 147:12-20						
I'll Praise My Maker While I've Breath	60		123			
Morning Has Broken	145	354	370			186
Rejoice, Ye Pure in Heart (Marion)	160		130			
Rejoice, Ye Pure in Heart (Vineyard Haven)	161					
See How Great a Flame Aspires	541		248			
Someone Asked the Question				2144		
Thou Art Worthy				2041		

Scripture Hymn Title	UMH	MVPC	CLUW	TFWS	SOZ	URW
Ephesians 1:3-14						
Amazing Grace! How Sweet the Sound	378	203	94		211	
Baptized in Water				2248		
Blessed Assurance, Jesus Is Mine!	369	65	287			
Child of Blessing, Child of Promise	611		232			
Children of the Heavenly Father	141		335			
Come, Thou Fount of Every Blessing	400	42	127			92
Father, We Thank You (ALBRIGHT)	563					
Father, We Thank You (RENDEZ À DIEU)	565					
Forward Through the Ages	555					
Glory to God in the Highest				2276		
Grace Greater than Our Sin	365					
Hail, Thou Once Despised Jesus	325					
He Who Began a Good Work in You				2163		
Holy Spirit, Truth Divine	465					
Holy, Holy				2039		
I'm Gonna Live So God Can Use Me				2153		
It Is Well with My Soul (When Peace, Like a River, Attendeth My Way)	377	250	304		20	
Jesus Our Friend and Brother	659					
Lord, Have Mercy	482					
Loving Spirit				2123		203
Morning Glory, Starlit Sky	194					
My Tribute	99					
Nothing But the Blood	362					
There Are Some Things I May Not Know				2147		
There Is a Fountain Filled with Blood	622					
There's a Wideness in God's Mercy	121					
Victory in Jesus	370		92			
We Are God's People				2220		
What Can Wash Away My Sin	362					
John 1:(1-9), 10-18						
At the Name of Jesus Every Knee Shall Bow	168					
Blessed Jesus, at Thy Word	596		108			
Break Forth, O Beauteous Heavenly Light	223					
Christ Is the World's Light	188					
Christ the Eternal Lord					94	

Scripture Hymn Title	UMH	MVPC	CLUW	TFWS	SOZ	URW
Christ the Lord Is Risen				2116		
Christ, Whose Glory Fills the Skies	173		281			
Cold December Flies Away	233					
Come and Seek the Ways of Wisdom						99
Come, Thou Almighty King	61	11				
Gather Us In				2236		54
Give Thanks to the Source						126
Go, Tell It on the Mountain	251	97			75	
Good Christian Friends, Rejoice	224		155			
Hail, Thou Once Despised Jesus	325					
Hark! the Herald Angels Sing	240	101				
I Sing the Almighty Power of God	152		65			
I Want to Walk as a Child of the Light	206		102			
I Was There to Hear Your Borning Cry				2051		
Infant Holy, Infant Lowly	229	116	152			
Jesus, Joy of Our Desiring	644		344			
Jesus, Name above All Names				2071		
Joy to the World, the Lord Is Come!	246	100	161			
Just a Closer Walk with Thee				2158	46	
Light of the World				2204		
Lord of the Dance (I Danced in the Morning)	261	128	170			
Lord, I Lift Your Name on High				2088		
Love Came Down at Christmas	242					
Morning Has Broken	145	354	370			186
Mothering God, You Gave Me Birth				2050		
Now It Is Evening				2187		
Now, on Land and Sea Descending	685		372			
O Come, All Ye Faithful	234	106				
O Holy Spirit, Root of Life				2121		79
O Love that Wilt Not Let Me Go	480	255	322			
O Love, How Deep, How Broad, How High	267					
O Morning Star, How Fair and Bright	247					
O Word of God Incarnate	598					
Of the Father's Love Begotten	184	52	66			
On This Day Earth Shall Ring	248					
Once in Royal David's City	250		159			
Savior of the Nations, Come	214					

Scripture Hymn Title	UMH	MVPC	CLUW	TFWS	SOZ	URW
Send Your Word	195		113			
Shine, Jesus, Shine			264	2173		
Sing of Mary, Pure and Lowly	272					
Source and Sovereign, Rock and Cloud	113					
That Boy-Child of Mary	241					
Thou Art Worthy				2041		
Thou Didst Leave Thy Throne			172	2100		
We Are Singing\We Are Marching\Siyahamba				2235		
What Feast of Love						119
When Christmas Morn Is Dawning	232					
Womb of Life				2046		
Word of God, Come Down on Earth	182					
This Is the Feast of Victory	638					
We Shall Overcome	533		140		127	
We Will Glorify the King of Kings				2087		
When All Is Ended						133
You Who Are Thirsty				2132		

January 6, 2009 (Epiphany of the Lord)

Liturgical Color: White

Scripture Hymn Title	UMH	MVPC	CLUW	TFWS	SOZ	URW
Isaiah 60:1-6						
Arise, Shine				2005		
Arise, Shine Out, Your Light Has Come	725					
Arise, Your Light Is Come						138
Break Forth, O Beauteous Heavenly Light	223					
De Tierra Lejana Venimos	243					
From a Distant Home	243					
Gather Us In				2236		54
Glory to God				2033		
Honor and Praise				2018		
Immortal, Invisible, God Only Wise	103		74			
Light of the World				2204		
O Morning Star, How Fair and Bright	247					
O Splendor of God's Glory Bright	679					211
Rise Up, O Men of God	576					
Rise, Shine, You People	187					
Shine, Jesus, Shine			264	2173		
There's a Song in the Air	249					
This Little Light of Mine	585		338		132	
We Are Called				2172		
We've a Story to Tell to the Nations	569					
Psalm 72:1-7, 10-14						
Blessed Be the Name of the Lord				2034		
Canticle of Simeon, Response	225					
Hail to the Lord's Anointed	203	81				
Here Am I				2178		

Scripture Hymn Title	UMH	MVPC	CLUW	TFWS	SOZ	URW
Holy Spirit, Come to Us				2118		395
Jesus Shall Reign Where'er the Sun	157					
Lead Me, Guide Me				2214		
My Soul Gives Glory to My God	198					
O Morning Star, How Fair and Bright	247					
Praise to the Lord				2029		309
Sing a New Song to the Lord				2045		
Song of Hope				2186		
Tell Out, My Soul, the Greatness of the Lord!	200					
There's a Song in the Air	249					
When God Restored Our Common Life				2182		
Why Stand So Far Away, My God?				2180		
Word of God, Come Down on Earth	182					
Wounded World that Cries for Healing				2177		

Ephesians 3:1-12

Scripture Hymn Title	UMH	MVPC	CLUW	TFWS	SOZ	URW
Blessed Assurance, Jesus Is Mine!	369	65	287			
Christ Is Made the Sure Foundation	559					
Christ Is the World's Light	188					
Christ, from Whom All Blessings Flow	550		250			
Go, Tell It on the Mountain	251	97				75
Grace Alone				2162		
Help Us Accept Each Other	560		253			
Make Me a Captive, Lord	421					
Song of Hope				2186		
We Are Called				2172		
We Are God's People				2220		
We Would See Jesus	256		168			
Ye Servants of God, Your Master Proclaim	181					

Matthew 2:1-12

Scripture Hymn Title	UMH	MVPC	CLUW	TFWS	SOZ	URW
'Twas in the Moon of Wintertime	244					
Alleluia	186		355			
Angels from the Realms of Glory	220					
Angels We Have Heard on High	238	98				
Break Forth, O Beauteous Heavenly Light	223					
Carol of the Epiphany				2094		
Child So Lovely, Here I Kneel Before You (Niño Lindo, Ante Ti Me Rindo)	222	114				

Scripture	Hymn Title	UMH	MVPC	CLUW	TFWS	SOZ	URW
	De Tierra Lejana Venimos	243					
	From a Distant Home	243					
	Give Thanks			247	2036		
	Go, Tell It on the Mountain	251	97			75	
	Honor and Praise				2018		
	In the Bleak Midwinter	221					
	Jesus Be Praised				2079		
	Lo, How a Rose E'er Blooming	216					
	O Little Town of Bethlehem	230	94				
	O Morning Star, How Fair and Bright	247					
	O the Depth of Love Divine	627					
	On This Day Earth Shall Ring	248					
	Rise Up, Shepherd, and Follow				2096		
	Sing We Now of Christmas	237		166			
	Star-Child				2095		
	The First Noel the Angel Did Say	245	89				
	The Virgin Mary Had a Baby Boy				2098		
	There's a Song in the Air	249					
	We Three Kings of Orient Are	254	108				
	We Would See Jesus	256		168			
	What Child Is This	219	112	154			
	When the Poor Ones (Cuando El Pobre)	434	301	138			
	Where Cross the Crowded Ways of Life	427	296				
	Wounded World that Cries for Healing				2177		

January 11, 2009 (Baptism of the Lord)

Liturgical Color: White

Scripture Hymn Title	UMH	MVPC	CLUW	TFWS	SOZ	URW
Genesis 1:1-5						
All Creatures of Our God and King	62	22				
All People that on Earth Do Dwell	75		118			
All Things Bright and Beautiful	147		63			
As Man and Woman We Were Made	642					
At the Name of Jesus Every Knee Shall Bow	168					
Bring Many Names				2047		
Enemy of Apathy						165
Eternal Father, Strong to Save				2191		
For the Beauty of the Earth	92	8				
For the Healing of the Nations	428					
God Created Heaven and Earth	151					
God of Many Names	105					
God of the Sparrow God of the Whale	122	37	59			
God the Sculptor of the Mountains				2060		
God, that Madest Earth and Heaven	688		374			
God, Who Stretched the Spangled Heavens	150		64			84
God, Whose Love Is Reigning o'er Us	100		73			74
How Great Thou Art	77	2	61			
I Sing the Almighty Power of God	152		65			
I'll Praise My Maker While I've Breath	60		123			
Joyful, Joyful, We Adore Thee	89	5	75			65
Jubilate, Servite				2017		383
Let All Things Now Living				2008		
Let Us with a Joyful Mind				2012		
Let's Sing Unto the Lord (Cantemos al Señor)	149	49	67			
Loving Spirit				2123		203

Scripture Hymn Title	UMH	MVPC	CLUW	TFWS	SOZ	URW
Many and Great, O God, Are Thy Things	148	50	71			232
Morning Has Broken	145	354	370			186
Mothering God, You Gave Me Birth				2050		
O God Who Shaped Creation	443					
She Comes Sailing on the Wind				2122		
Shine, Jesus, Shine			264	2173		
Spirit of God				2117		
Spirit, Spirit of Gentleness				2120		
This Is My Father's World	144	47	62			71
Thou Art Worthy				2041		
Water Has Held Us						187
We, Thy People, Praise Thee	67		72			
Wind Who Makes All Winds that Blow	538					
Womb of Life				2046		

Psalm 29

Scripture Hymn Title	UMH	MVPC	CLUW	TFWS	SOZ	URW
Awesome God				2040		
Blessed Be the Name of the Lord				2034		
Father, I Adore You			225	2038		
Gloria, Gloria	72		353			380
Glory to God				2033		
God of the Sparrow God of the Whale	122	37	59			
God Weeps				2048		
Great Is the Lord				2022		
Holy				2019		
Holy, Holy, Holy Lord				2256		
Holy, Holy, Holy! Lord God Almighty	64	4	79			
I Sing the Almighty Power of God	152		65			
I'll Praise My Maker While I've Breath	60		123			
Let All Things Now Living				2008		
Many and Great, O God, Are Thy Things	148	50	71			232
O Worship the King, All-Glorious Above	73					
Praise and Thanksgiving Be to God	604		230			
Praise to the Lord, the Almighty	139	29	68			63
Shout to the Lord				2074		
Source and Sovereign, Rock and Cloud	113					
We Sing of Your Glory				2011		
You Alone Are Holy				2077		

Scripture Hymn Title	UMH	MVPC	CLUW	TFWS	SOZ	URW
Acts 19:1-7						
Baptized in Water				2248		
Come, Holy Ghost, Our Souls Inspire	651					
Daw-Kee, Aim Daw-Tsi-Taw	330					
Holy Spirit, Come, Confirm Us	331		217			
O Spirit of the Living God	539					
Praise and Thanksgiving Be to God	604		230			
Sweet, Sweet Spirit	334	186	220			
Wash, O God, Our Sons and Daughters	605					
We Were Baptized in Christ Jesus				2251		
Mark 1:4-11						
At the Font We Start Our Journey				2114		
Blessed Be the God of Israel	209					12
Come, Be Baptized				2252		
Come, Holy Ghost, Our Souls Inspire	651					
Crashing Waters at Creation						105
Jesus, Name above All Names				2071		
Like the Murmur of the Dove's Song	544					
Loving Spirit				2123		203
More Precious than Silver				2065		
Praise and Thanksgiving Be to God	604		230			
She Comes Sailing on the Wind				2122		
Spirit of Faith, Come Down	332		219			
Spirit of God				2117		
Spirit of the Living God, Fall Afresh on Me	393	177	214		226	
Spirit Song	347	190	91			
Spirit, Now Live in Me						164
Spirit, Spirit of Gentleness				2120		
Spirit, Working in Creation						150
This Is the Spirit's Entry Now	608					
Thou Art Worthy				2041		
Water Has Held Us						187
When Jesus Came to Jordan	252	125				
You Have Put on Christ	609					

January 18, 2009 (Second Sunday after the Epiphany)

Liturgical Color: Green

Scripture Hymn Title	UMH	MVPC	CLUW	TFWS	SOZ	URW
1 Samuel 3:1-10 (11-20)						
Be Thou My Vision	451	240				180
Come, Thou Fount of Every Blessing	400	42	127			92
Faith, While Trees Are Still in Blossom	508		97			
God the Spirit, Guide and Guardian	648					
Here I Am, Lord (I, the Lord of Sea and Sky)	593	289	263			
How Shall They Hear the Word of God	649					
I Am Thine, O Lord	419	218				
Lord, Speak to Me, that I May Speak	463					
Make Me a Servant				2176		
Open My Eyes, that I May See	454	184				
The Summons				2130		60
Whom Shall I Send?	582					
Psalm 139:1-6, 13-18						
Creating God, Your Fingers Trace	109					
Dear Lord, Lead Me Day by Day	411	100				
Forth in Thy Name, O Lord, I Go	438					
God the Sculptor of the Mountains				2060		
Guide My Feet				2208		
How Like a Gentle Spirit	115		216			
I Was There to Hear Your Borning Cry				2051		
I'll Praise My Maker While I've Breath	60		123			
Immortal, Invisible, God Only Wise	103		74			
Lead Me, Guide Me				2214		
Loving Spirit				2123		203
Mothering God, You Gave Me Birth				2050		
Now Thank We All Our God	102					
Praise to the Lord, the Almighty	139	29	68			63
Sing Praise to God Who Reigns Above	126		60			70

41

Scripture Hymn Title	UMH	MVPC	CLUW	TFWS	SOZ	URW
The Care the Eagle Gives Her Young	118		302			199
The Lone, Wild Bird				2052		
Thou Hidden Love of God	414					
You Are Mine				2218		

1 Corinthians 6:12-20

	UMH	MVPC	CLUW	TFWS	SOZ	URW
Come Down, O Love Divine	475					
Come, Let Us with Our Lord Arise				2084		
Cry of My Heart				2165		
Dear Jesus, in Whose Life I See	468					
Holy Spirit, Truth Divine	465					
I Want a Principle Within	410					
Lord, Be Glorified				2150		
Nothing between My Soul and My Savior	373				21	
O For a Heart to Praise My God	417					
O Perfect Love, All Human Thought Transcending	645					
Sanctuary	2164					
Take Our Bread	640		238			
When We Are Living (Pues Si Vivimos)	356	337	310			175

John 1:43-51

	UMH	MVPC	CLUW	TFWS	SOZ	URW
Alleluia	186		355			
Be Thou My Vision	451	240				180
Come and See				2127		
Forward Through the Ages	555					
He Leadeth Me: O Blessed Thought	128	237				
I Am Thine, O Lord	419	218				
I Have Decided to Follow Jesus				2129		
Jesus Calls Us o'er the Tumult	398		96			
Lord, You Give the Great Commission	584					
O Jesus, I Have Promised	396	214				
O the Lamb, the Loving Lamb	300					
Rise Up, O Men of God	576					
The Summons				2130		60
Two Fishermen				2101		
We Are Climbing Jacob's Ladder	418		314		205	
Whom Shall I Send?	582					
Would I Have Answered When You Called				2137		
You Are Mine				2218		

January 25, 2009 (Third Sunday after the Epiphany)

Liturgical Color: Green

Scripture Hymn Title	UMH	MVPC	CLUW	TFWS	SOZ	URW
Jonah 3:1-5, 10						
Blessed Be the God of Israel	209					12
Come, All of You	350					
Depth of Mercy! Can There Be	355		273			
For the Healing of the Nations	428					
Forgive Us, Lord				2134		
Give Me a Clean Heart				2133	182	
Grace Greater than Our Sin	365					
I Surrender All	354	225			67	
I Will Call upon the Lord				2002		
In Christ There Is No East or West	548				65	
It's Me, It's Me, O Lord	352		326		110	
Marvelous Grace of Our Loving Lord	365					
O God Beyond All Praising				2009		
Rock of Ages, Cleft for Me	361	247				
Seek the Lord Who Now Is Present	124					
We Bring the Sacrifice of Praise				2031		
When the Church of Jesus Shuts Its Outer Door	592					
Where Charity and Love Prevail	549					
Your Love, O God	120	26				
Psalm 62:5-12						
Hope of the World	178					
I Will Call upon the Lord				2002		
I Will Trust in the Lord	464	292		14		
If Thou But Suffer God to Guide Thee	142					
Jesus, Savior, Lord (Saranam, Saranam)	523	105				

Scripture Hymn Title	UMH	MVPC	CLUW	TFWS	SOZ	URW
My Life Is in You, Lord				2032		
My Soul Is at Rest						387
O God, Our Help in Ages Past	117					200
O Lord, Hear My Prayer				2200		390
Praise the Name of Jesus				2066		
Shout to the Lord				2074		
Taste and See				2267		258
The First Song of Isaiah				2030		

1 Corinthians 7:29-31

Scripture Hymn Title	UMH	MVPC	CLUW	TFWS	SOZ	URW
Change My Heart, O God			278	2152		
Dear Lord, Lead Me Day by Day	411		100			
Forth in Thy Name, O Lord, I Go	438					
God of Grace and God of Glory	577	287				
I Want to Be Ready	722				151	
It's Me, It's Me, O Lord	352		326		110	
Living for Jesus				2149		
Seek Ye First the Kingdom of God	405	201	136			
Soon and Very Soon	706		385		198	
Take My Life, and Let It Be Consecrated	399		312			
Turn Your Eyes upon Jesus	349					

Mark 1:14-20

Scripture Hymn Title	UMH	MVPC	CLUW	TFWS	SOZ	URW
Blessed Be the God of Israel	209					12
Come and See				2127		
Come, All of You	350					
Cry of My Heart				2165		
Dear Lord and Father of Mankind	358					
Depth of Mercy! Can There Be	355		273			
Forth in Thy Name, O Lord, I Go	438					
God of Grace and God of Glory	577	287				
Great Lover, Calling Us to Share						80
I Can Hear My Savior Calling	338					
I Have Decided to Follow Jesus				2129		
Jesus Calls Us o'er the Tumult	398		96			
Lord God, Your Love Has Called Us Here	579					
Lord of the Dance (I Danced in the Morning)	261	128	170			
Lord, You Have Come to the Lakeshore	344	195	90			

Scripture	Hymn Title	UMH	MVPC	CLUW	TFWS	SOZ	URW
	O Jesus, I Have Promised	396	214				
	Praise the Name of Jesus				2066		
	Softly and Tenderly Jesus Is Calling	348	193	284			
	Sois la Semilla (You Are the Seed)	583	291				
	The Summons				2130		60
	Tú Has Venido a la Orilla	344					
	Two Fishermen				2101		
	Where He Leads Me	338				42	
	Would I Have Answered When You Called				2137		
	You Are Mine				2218		

February 1, 2009 (Fourth Sunday after the Epiphany)

Liturgical Color: Green

Scripture Hymn Title	UMH	MVPC	CLUW	TFWS	SOZ	URW
Deuteronomy 18:15-20						
All Creatures of Our God and King	62	22				
Awesome God				2040		
Close to Thee	407				7	
God Hath Spoken by the Prophets	108	38				
Guide Me, O Thou Great Jehovah	127					
He Leadeth Me: O Blessed Thought	128	237				
How Shall They Hear the Word of God	649					
Thou My Everlasting Portion	407					
We Sing of Your Glory				2011		
We Sing to You, O God				2001		293
Psalm 111						
All My Hope Is Firmly Grounded	132					
Amen, We Praise Your Name, O God (Amen Siakudumisa)				2067		398
Awesome God				2040		
Great Is the Lord				2022		
Great Is Thy Faithfulness	140	30	81			
I'll Praise My Maker While I've Breath	60		123			
In the Lord I'll Be Ever Thankful				2195		381
Nothing Can Trouble				2054		388
O Holy Spirit, Root of Life				2121		79
O Master, Let Me Walk with Thee	430		315			
O Worship the King, All-Glorious Above	73					
Praise the Lord Who Reigns Above	96		124			
Praise the Source of Faith and Learning				2004		
Sing Praise to God Who Reigns Above	126		60			70

Scripture Hymn Title	UMH	MVPC	CLUW	TFWS	SOZ	URW
Thank You, Lord	84				228	
Thou Art Worthy				2041		
We, Thy People, Praise Thee	67		72			
What a Mighty God We Serve				2021		

1 Corinthians 8:1-13

	UMH	MVPC	CLUW	TFWS	SOZ	URW
All Creatures of Our God and King	62	22				
All Praise to Our Redeeming Lord	554					
Baptized in Water				2248		
Be Thou My Vision	451	240				180
Blest Be the Tie that Binds	557	347				
Christ Is the World's Light	188					
Draw Us in the Spirit's Tether	632					
God Created Heaven and Earth	151					
God Made from One Blood				2170		
Jesus, Lord, We Look to Thee	562					
Jesus, United by Thy Grace	561					
Now It Is Evening				2187		
O Christ, the Healer, We Have Come	265					
Take Our Bread	640		238			
Together We Serve				2175		
We Believe in One True God	85					

Mark 1:21-28

	UMH	MVPC	CLUW	TFWS	SOZ	URW
An Outcast Among Outcasts				2104		
Awesome God				2040		
Christ, Whose Glory Fills the Skies	173		281			
Heal Me, Hands of Jesus	262					
Majesty, Worship His Majesty	176	171	204			
O Christ, the Healer, We Have Come	265					
Rise, Shine, You People	187					
Silence, Frenzied, Unclean Spirit	264					
To Know You More				2161		
What a Mighty God We Serve				2021		
When Jesus the Healer Passed Through Galilee	263		171			
Wounded World that Cries for Healing				2177		

February 8, 2009 (Fifth Sunday after the Epiphany)

Liturgical Color: Green

Scripture Hymn Title	UMH	MVPC	CLUW	TFWS	SOZ	URW
Isaiah 40:21-31						
A Mighty Fortress Is Our God	110	25				271
Arise, Your Light Is Come						138
Come, Let Us Join Our Friends Above	709		387			
God of the Ages	698	377				
Holy Ground				2272		
How Like a Gentle Spirit	115		216			
In the Midst of New Dimensions				2238		
Jesus Is All the World to Me	469	234			216	
Lord, We Come to Ask Your Blessing				2230		
Many and Great, O God, Are Thy Things	148	50	71			232
May You Run and Not Be Weary				2281		451
O Holy Spirit, Root of Life				2121		79
On Eagle's Wings	143		83			
People Need the Lord				2244		
Praise to the Lord, the Almighty	139	29	68			63
Praise, My Soul, the King of Heaven	66					75
Spirit of God				2117		
The Care the Eagle Gives Her Young	118		302			199
Those Who Wait on the Lord						435
What a Friend We Have in Jesus	526	257	333			
You Alone Are Holy				2077		
Psalm 147:1-11, 20c						
Give Thanks			247	2036		
God of the Sparrow God of the Whale	122	37	59			
Great Is the Lord				2022		
Holy Ground				2272		

Scripture Hymn Title	UMH	MVPC	CLUW	TFWS	SOZ	URW
I Love You, Lord				2068		
I'm Goin'a Sing When the Spirit Says Sing	333		223		81	
Jesus Is All the World to Me	469	234			216	
Lord, I Lift Your Name on High				2088		
May You Run and Not Be Weary				2281		451
Mil Voces Para Celebrar	59					
O For a Thousand Tongues to Sing	57	1	226			
Praise to the Lord, the Almighty	139	29	68			63
Rejoice, Ye Pure in Heart (MARION)	160		130			
Rejoice, Ye Pure in Heart (VINEYARD HAVEN)	161					
Someone Asked the Question				2144		
What a Friend We Have in Jesus	526	257	333			

1 Corinthians 9:16-23

Scripture Hymn Title	UMH	MVPC	CLUW	TFWS	SOZ	URW
A Charge to Keep I Have	413					
Christ for the World We Sing	568		260			
Gather Us In				2236		54
Give Me the Faith Which Can Remove	650					
God of Love and God of Power	578					
I Want a Principle Within	410					
Lord of the Dance (I Danced in the Morning)	261	128	170			
Make Me a Captive, Lord	421					
Make Me a Servant				2176		
People Need the Lord				2244		

Mark 1:29-39

Scripture Hymn Title	UMH	MVPC	CLUW	TFWS	SOZ	URW
Amen, Amen				2072		
Dear Lord and Father of Mankind	358					
Give Thanks			247	2036		
Heal Me, Hands of Jesus	262					
Healer of Our Every Ill				2213		161
I'm So Glad Jesus Lifted Me				2151		
Jesus Is All the World to Me	469	234			216	
Lord of the Dance (I Danced in the Morning)	261	128	170			
Lord, Listen to Your Children				2207		
Lord, We Come to Ask Your Blessing				2230		
Mil Voces Para Celebrar	59					
O Christ, the Healer, We Have Come	265					

Scripture Hymn Title	UMH	MVPC	CLUW	TFWS	SOZ	URW
O For a Thousand Tongues to Sing	57	1	226			
O Lord, You're Beautiful				2064		
O Sabbath Rest of Galilee	499					
Oh, I Know the Lord's Laid His Hands on Me				2139		
People Need the Lord				2244		
Precious Lord, Take My Hand	474		309		179	
Send Me, Lord	497		331			
Serenity	499					
Silence, Frenzied, Unclean Spirit	264					
Take Time to Be Holy	395					
There Is a Balm in Gilead	375	262	98		123	
We've a Story to Tell to the Nations	569					
What a Friend We Have in Jesus	526	257	333			
When Jesus the Healer Passed Through Galilee	263		171			
Word of God, Come Down on Earth	182					

February 15, 2009 (Sixth Sunday after the Epiphany)

Liturgical Color: Green

Scripture Hymn Title	UMH	MVPC	CLUW	TFWS	SOZ	URW
2 Kings 5:1-14						
Come, Ye Sinners, Poor and Needy	340					
Gather Us In				2236		54
Heal Us, Emmanuel, Hear Our Prayer	266		328			
Honor and Praise				2018		
I've Just Come from the Fountain				2250		
O Christ, the Healer, We Have Come	265					
Praise to the Lord, the Almighty	139	29	68			63
Praise, My Soul, the King of Heaven	66					75
Spirit of the Living God, Fall Afresh on Me	393	177	214		226	
The God of Abraham Praise	116	28				
Wash, O God, Our Sons and Daughters	605					
Water, River, Spirit, Grace				2253		
We, Thy People, Praise Thee	67		72			
Psalm 30						
Amazing Grace! How Sweet the Sound	378	203	94		211	
Beams of Heaven as I Go	524				10	
Camina, Pueblo de Dios (Walk On, O People of God)	305	151				
Come, We that Love the Lord (MARCHING TO ZION)	733				3	139
Come, We that Love the Lord (ST. THOMAS)	732					
Come, Ye Disconsolate, Where'er Ye Languish	510					
Faith Is Patience in the Night				2211		
Give Thanks			247	2036		
Hymn of Promise (In the Bulb There Is a Flower)	707	338	392			

51

Scripture Hymn Title	UMH	MVPC	CLUW	TFWS	SOZ	URW
I'll Fly Away				2282	183	
In the Lord I'll Be Ever Thankful				2195		381
It Is Well with My Soul (When Peace, Like a River, Attendeth My Way)	377	250	304		20	
Joy Comes with the Dawn				2210		
Joy in the Morning				2284		
O Freedom				2194		
O Love that Wilt Not Let Me Go	480	255	322			
Praise, My Soul, the King of Heaven	66					75
Someone Asked the Question				2144		
Soon and Very Soon	706		385		198	
Thank You, Lord	84				228	
What Does the Lord Require of You				2174		
You Have Turned Our Sadness (Psalm 30)						255

1 Corinthians 9:24-27

Scripture Hymn Title	UMH	MVPC	CLUW	TFWS	SOZ	URW
A Charge to Keep I Have	413					
Close to Thee	407				7	
Come, Let Us Join Our Friends Above	709		387			
Cry of My Heart				2165		
Faith Is Patience in the Night				2211		
Guide My Feet				2208		
I Need Thee Every Hour	397					
May You Run and Not Be Weary				2281		451
Soon and Very Soon	706		385		198	
Thou Hidden Love of God	414					
Thou My Everlasting Portion	407					
Through It All	507		279			
Turn Your Eyes upon Jesus	349					
What Does the Lord Require of You				2174		
When We All Get to Heaven (Sing the Wondrous Love of Jesus)	701	383	381		15	

Mark 1:40-45

Scripture Hymn Title	UMH	MVPC	CLUW	TFWS	SOZ	URW
He Touched Me (Shackled by a Heavy Burden)	367	209	286		72	
Heal Us, Emmanuel, Hear Our Prayer	266		328			
Jesus' Hands Were Kind Hands	273		176			

Scripture Hymn Title	UMH	MVPC	CLUW	TFWS	SOZ	URW
Just as I Am, Without One Plea	357				208	
May You Run and Not Be Weary				2281		451
My Hope Is Built on Nothing Less	368	261				
Nothing But the Blood	362					
O Christ, the Healer, We Have Come	265					
O Happy Day, that Fixed My Choice	391					
O Lord, You're Beautiful				2064		
Oh, I Know the Lord's Laid His Hands on Me				2139		
People Need the Lord				2244		
Since Jesus Came into My Heart				2140		
There's a Song				2141		
Turn Your Eyes upon Jesus	349					
Wellspring of Wisdom	506					173
What Can Wash Away My Sin	362					
When Jesus the Healer Passed Through Galilee	263		171			

February 22, 2009 (Transfiguration)

Liturgical Color: White

Scripture Hymn Title	UMH	MVPC	CLUW	TFWS	SOZ	URW
2 Kings 2:1-12						
All Hail King Jesus				2069		
Arise, Shine				2005		
Awesome God				2040		
Canticle of Remembrance	652					
Children of the Heavenly Father	141		335			
Come, Holy Ghost, Our Hearts Inspire	603		218			
Come, Holy Ghost, Our Souls Inspire	651					
Hail to the Lord's Anointed	203	81				
He Is Exalted				2070		
Honor and Praise				2018		
How Great Thou Art	77	2	61			
Source and Sovereign, Rock and Cloud	113					
Steal Away to Jesus	704		378		134	
Swing Low, Sweet Chariot	703		384		104	
Psalm 50:1-6						
From the Rising of the Sun				2024		
Holy, Holy, Holy! Lord God Almighty	64	4	79			
Immortal, Invisible, God Only Wise	103		74			
O Morning Star, How Fair and Bright	247					
Praise to the Lord				2029		309
Seek the Lord Who Now Is Present	124					
Shine, Jesus, Shine			264	2173		
Source and Sovereign, Rock and Cloud	113					
2 Corinthians 4:3-6						
All Hail King Jesus				2069		
As a Fire Is Meant for Burning				2237		
Canticle of Light and Darkness	205					

Scripture	Hymn Title	UMH	MVPC	CLUW	TFWS	SOZ	URW
	Christ Beside Me				2166		
	Christ Is the World's Light	188					
	Christ, Whose Glory Fills the Skies	173		281			
	He Is Exalted				2070		
	I Want to Walk as a Child of the Light	206		102			
	Light of the World				2204		
	O Gladsome Light	686					
	O Morning Star, How Fair and Bright	247					
	Open My Eyes, that I May See	454	184				
	Open Our Eyes				2086		
	Shine, Jesus, Shine			264	2173		
	Source and Sovereign, Rock and Cloud	113					
	Spirit of Faith, Come Down	332		219			
	This Little Light of Mine	585		338		132	
	Turn Your Eyes upon Jesus	349					
	You Are Mine				2218		

Mark 9:2-9

Scripture	Hymn Title	UMH	MVPC	CLUW	TFWS	SOZ	URW
	All Hail King Jesus				2069		
	Arise, Shine				2005		
	As We Gather at Your Table				2268		
	Christ Is the World's Light	188					
	Christ, upon the Mountain Peak	260					
	Christ, Whose Glory Fills the Skies	173		281			
	Christian People, Raise Your Song	636					
	Come, Let Us with Our Lord Arise				2084		
	Hail to the Lord's Anointed	203	81				
	He Is Exalted				2070		
	Honor and Praise				2018		
	I Stand Amazed in the Presence	371		93			
	Majesty, Worship His Majesty	176	171	204			
	O Morning Star, How Fair and Bright	247					
	O Wondrous Sight! O Vision Fair	258		169			
	Shine, Jesus, Shine			264	2173		
	Swiftly Pass the Clouds of Glory				2102		
	This Is the Feast of Victory	638					
	Turn Your Eyes upon Jesus	349					
	We Have Come at Christ's Own Bidding				2103		
	You Alone Are Holy				2077		
	You, Lord, Are Both Lamb and Shepherd						98

February 25, 2009 (Ash Wednesday)

Liturgical Color: Purple

Scripture Hymn Title	UMH	MVPC	CLUW	TFWS	SOZ	URW
Joel 2:1-2, 12-17						
All Who Love and Serve Your City	433					
Blow Ye the Trumpet, Blow	379	309				
Forgive Us, Lord				2134		
Lord, I Want to Be a Christian	402	215			76	
My Lord, What a Morning	719		386		145	
Sanctuary				2164		
See How Great a Flame Aspires	541		248			
Sing, My Tongue, the Glorious Battle	296					
There's a Wideness in God's Mercy	121					
Weary of All Trumpeting	442					
Without Seeing You				2206		
Psalm 51:1-17						
Bread of the World in Mercy Broken	624		240			
Breathe on Me, Breath of God	420					167
Change My Heart, O God			278	2152		
Come and Fill Our Hearts				2157		378
Create in Me (Psalm 51)						275
Depth of Mercy! Can There Be	355		273			
Fix Me, Jesus	655				122	
Forgive Us, Lord				2134		
Give Me a Clean Heart				2133	182	
Great Lover, Calling Us to Share						80
Have Thine Own Way, Lord!	382	213	327			
I Want a Principle Within	410					
Jesus, Lover of My Soul	479					
Jubilate, Servite				2017		383

Scripture Hymn Title	UMH	MVPC	CLUW	TFWS	SOZ	URW
Just a Closer Walk with Thee				2158	46	
Just as I Am, Without One Plea	357					208
Kyrie				2275		
Let Us Pray to the Lord	485					
Lord, Have Mercy				2277		
Mil Voces Para Celebrar	59					
O For a Heart to Praise My God	417					
O For a Thousand Tongues to Sing	57	1	226			
Open My Eyes, that I May See	454	184				
Open Our Eyes				2086		
Out of the Depths I Cry to You	515					
Pass Me Not, O Gentle Savior	351		271			
Please Enter My Heart, Hosanna				2154		
Since Jesus Came into My Heart				2140		
Sunday's Palms Are Wednesday's Ashes				2138		
The Sacrifice You Accept (Psalm 51)						276
Thy Holy Wings, O Savior	502					

2 Corinthians 5:20b–6:10

Scripture Hymn Title	UMH	MVPC	CLUW	TFWS	SOZ	URW
Alas! and Did My Savior Bleed (MARTYRDOM)	294					
Alas! and Did My Savior Bleed (HUDSON)	359	202			8	
Close to Thee	407				7	
Come Back Quickly to the Lord	343		272			
Come, Every Soul by Sin Oppressed	337					
Creator of the Earth and Skies	450					
Cry of My Heart				2165		
Depth of Mercy! Can There Be	355		273			
Give Me the Faith Which Can Remove	650					
Holy Spirit, Truth Divine	465					
I Want a Principle Within	410					
In the Singing				2255		
In Thee Is Gladness	169					
Lead On, O Cloud of Presence				2234		
Lead On, O King Eternal	580	174				
Let Us Plead for Faith Alone	385					
Love Divine, All Loves Excelling	384					100
More Like You				2167		
Morning Glory, Starlit Sky	194					

Scripture Hymn Title	UMH	MVPC	CLUW	TFWS	SOZ	URW
O For a Heart to Praise My God	417					
O the Depth of Love Divine	627					
Only Trust Him	337					
Spirit of God, Descend upon My Heart	500					
Stand Up, Stand Up for Jesus	514					
The Church's One Foundation	546					
The Church's One Foundation	545	269	255			
There Are Some Things I May Not Know				2147		
Thou My Everlasting Portion	407					
We Walk by Faith				2196		
What Wondrous Love Is This	292					
Ye Servants of God, Your Master Proclaim	181					

Matthew 6:1-6, 16-21

Scripture Hymn Title	UMH	MVPC	CLUW	TFWS	SOZ	URW
Come and Find the Quiet Center				2128		
Come Away with Me				2202		59
Daw-Kee, Aim Daw-Tsi-Taw	330					
God, How Can We Forgive				2169		
He Never Said a Mumbalin' Word	291				101	
I'm So Glad Jesus Lifted Me				2151		
It's Me, It's Me, O Lord	352		326		110	
Jesus, We Are Here				2273		
Just as I Am, Without One Plea	357				208	
Let Us Plead for Faith Alone	385					
Lord, I Want to Be a Christian	402	215			76	
Lord, Who Throughout These Forty Days	269	181				
Love Divine, All Loves Excelling	384					100
More Love to Thee, O Christ	453	318				
Near to the Heart of God (There Is a Place of Quiet Rest)	472	324				
O Sabbath Rest of Galilee	499					
Open Our Eyes				2086		
Prayer Is the Soul's Sincere Desire	492					
Prayers of the People				2201		
Serenity	499					
Since Jesus Came into My Heart				2140		
Sunday's Palms Are Wednesday's Ashes				2138		

Scripture Hymn Title	UMH	MVPC	CLUW	TFWS	SOZ	URW
Sweet Hour of Prayer	496	248	330			
Take Time to Be Holy	395					
The Fragrance of Christ				2205		
The Lord's Prayer				2278		453

March 1, 2009 (First Sunday in Lent)

Liturgical Color: Purple

Scripture Hymn Title	UMH	MVPC	CLUW	TFWS	SOZ	URW
Genesis 9:8-17						
As a Fire Is Meant for Burning				2237		
Children of the Heavenly Father	141		335			
Faith, While Trees Are Still in Blossom	508		97			
Give to the Winds Thy Fears	129		282			
God Made from One Blood				2170		
God of the Sparrow God of the Whale	122	37	59			
Great Is Thy Faithfulness	140	30	81			
In the Midst of New Dimensions				2238		
Let All Things Now Living				2008		
Let Us with a Joyful Mind				2012		
O Love that Wilt Not Let Me Go	480	255	322			
There's a Wideness in God's Mercy	121					
Thy Holy Wings, O Savior	502					
Water Has Held Us						187
Psalm 25:1-10						
Be Thou My Vision	451	240				180
Cry of My Heart				2165		
Dear Lord, Lead Me Day by Day	411		100			
Holy Ground				2272		
How Like a Gentle Spirit	115		216			
I Want a Principle Within	410					
In Remembrance of Me				2254		
Jesus, Name above All Names				2071		
Lead Me, Guide Me				2214		
Lead Me, Lord	473					226
Lift Every Voice and Sing	519				32	

Scripture Hymn Title	UMH	MVPC	CLUW	TFWS	SOZ	URW
More Like You				2167		
Please Enter My Heart, Hosanna				2154		
To Know You More				2161		

1 Peter 3:18-22

Scripture Hymn Title	UMH	MVPC	CLUW	TFWS	SOZ	URW
Ah, Holy Jesus, How Hast Thou Offended	289		186			
Alas! and Did My Savior Bleed (Martyrdom)	294					
Alas! and Did My Savior Bleed (Hudson)	359	202			8	
As the Deer			116	2025		267
Christ the Lord Is Risen Today	302	152	193			
Come, Be Baptized				2252		
Come, Thou Almighty King	61	11				
Hail, Thou Once Despised Jesus	325					
I Stand Amazed in the Presence	371		93			
Lord, I Lift Your Name on High				2088		
My Song Is Love Unknown				2083		
Rejoice, the Lord Is King (Darwall's 148th)	715					
Rejoice, the Lord Is King (Gopsal)	716					
Spirit Song	347	190	91			
Thy Holy Wings, O Savior	502					
Wash, O God, Our Sons and Daughters	605					
Water, River, Spirit, Grace				2253		
We Know that Christ Is Raised	610		231			
We Were Baptized in Christ Jesus				2251		
Wonder of Wonders				2247		

Mark 1:9-15

Scripture Hymn Title	UMH	MVPC	CLUW	TFWS	SOZ	URW
Come, Be Baptized				2252		
Come, Sinners, to the Gospel Feast *Communion*	616					
Come, Thou Almighty King	61	11				
Crashing Waters at Creation						105
Holy Ground				2272		
I Want Jesus to Walk with Me	521		104		95	110
Jesus Walked This Lonesome Valley				2112		
Jesus, Name above All Names				2071		
Jesus, Tempted in the Desert				2105		
Like the Murmur of the Dove's Song	544					
Lord, Who Throughout These Forty Days	269		181			

Scripture Hymn Title	UMH	MVPC	CLUW	TFWS	SOZ	URW
O Jesus, I Have Promised	396	214				
O Love, How Deep, How Broad, How High	267					
Precious Name	536					
She Comes Sailing on the Wind				2122		
Spirit of God				2117		
Spirit Song	347	190	91			
Spirit, Now Live in Me						164
Spirit, Working in Creation						150
Take the Name of Jesus with You	536					
Take Time to Be Holy	395					
This Is the Spirit's Entry Now	608					
Water Has Held Us						187
We'll Understand It Better By and By	525	317			55	
When Jesus Came to Jordan	252	125				
Wild and Lone the Prophet's Voice				2089		
Wonder of Wonders				2247		

March 8, 2009 (Second Sunday in Lent)

Liturgical Color: Purple

Scripture Hymn Title	UMH	MVPC	CLUW	TFWS	SOZ	URW
Genesis 17:1-7, 15-16						
Be Thou My Vision	451	240				180
Children of the Heavenly Father	141		335			
Cry of My Heart				2165		
El Shaddai	123	45	77			
Faith, While Trees Are Still in Blossom	508		97			
God, Whose Love Is Reigning o'er Us	100		73			74
Great Is Thy Faithfulness	140	30	81			
Lead Me, Lord	473					226
My Tribute	99					
Stand Up and Bless the Lord	662		128			
The God of Abraham Praise	116	28				
To Know You More				2161		
You Alone Are Holy				2077		
Psalm 22:23-31						
All People that on Earth Do Dwell	75		118			
Angels from the Realms of Glory	220					
Give Thanks			247	2036		
Glory to God				2033		
How Majestic Is Your Name				2023		
I'll Praise My Maker While I've Breath	60		123			
O Worship the King, All-Glorious Above	73					
Praise the Lord Who Reigns Above	96		124			
Praise to the Lord				2029		309
Praise, My Soul, the King of Heaven	66					75
The God of Abraham Praise	116	28				
We Sing of Your Glory				2011		
You Satisfy the Hungry Heart	629					

Scripture Hymn Title	UMH	MVPC	CLUW	TFWS	SOZ	URW
Romans 4:13-25						
Be Still, My Soul	534		307			
Be Thou My Vision	451	240				180
Faith Is Patience in the Night				2211		
Faith of Our Fathers	710	385				
Faith, While Trees Are Still in Blossom	508		97			
Grace Alone				2162		
Here Is Bread, Here Is Wine				2266		
In the Singing				2255		
Let Us Plead for Faith Alone	385					
Lord, I Lift Your Name on High				2088		
My Hope Is Built on Nothing Less	368	261				
My Life Is in You, Lord				2032		
See How Great a Flame Aspires	541		248			
Sing Alleluia to the Lord				2258		404
Standing on the Promises of Christ My King	374	252				
There Are Some Things I May Not Know				2147		
Through It All	507		279			
We Walk by Faith				2196		
Mark 8:31-38						
All I Need Is You				2080		
And Are We Yet Alive	553					
Be Thou My Vision	451	240				180
Beneath the Cross of Jesus	297					
Come, Ye Thankful People, Come	694		241			
Faith, While Trees Are Still in Blossom	508		97			
Father, I Adore You			225	2038		
Forth in Thy Name, O Lord, I Go	438					
Hail, Thou Once Despised Jesus	325					
I Can Hear My Savior Calling	338					
I Have Decided to Follow Jesus				2129		
Jesus Calls Us o'er the Tumult	398		96			
Jesus, Draw Me Close				2159		
Lift High the Cross	159	164	174			
Lord of the Dance (I Danced in the Morning)	261	128	170			
Lord, Have Mercy				2277		
Must Jesus Bear the Cross Alone	424					

Scripture Hymn Title	UMH	MVPC	CLUW	TFWS	SOZ	URW
My Song Is Love Unknown				2083		
Rejoice, Ye Pure in Heart (MARION)	160		130			
Rejoice, Ye Pure in Heart (VINEYARD HAVEN)	161					
Take Up Thy Cross, the Savior Said	415		145			
The Church of Christ, in Every Age	589					
The God of Abraham Praise	116	28				
The Summons				2130		60
Weary of All Trumpeting	442					
Where He Leads Me	338				42	

March 15, 2009 (Third Sunday in Lent)

Liturgical Color: Purple

Scripture Hymn Title	UMH	MVPC	CLUW	TFWS	SOZ	URW
Exodus 20:1-17						
Change My Heart, O God			278	2152		
Come! Come! Everybody Worship				2271		
Cry of My Heart				2165		
God Made from One Blood				2170		
I Want a Principle Within	410					
If Thou But Suffer God to Guide Thee	142					
Jaya Ho (Victory Hymn)	478					
Lead Me, Lord	473					226
Lord, We Come to Ask Your Blessing				2230		
Love the Lord Your God				2168		
Make Me a Captive, Lord	421					
Move Me, Move Me	471		357		185	
O Come, O Come, Emmanuel	211	80				
O For a Heart to Praise My God	417					
Trust and Obey (When We Walk with the Lord)	467		320			
You Alone Are Holy				2077		
Psalm 19						
Alleluia	186		355			
As the Deer			116	2025		267
Awesome God				2040		
Creating God, Your Fingers Trace						67
For the Music of Creation						64
From All that Dwell Below the Skies	101		126			
God Created Heaven and Earth	151					
God, Who Stretched the Spangled Heavens	150		64			84

Scripture Hymn Title	UMH	MVPC	CLUW	TFWS	SOZ	URW
Great Is the Lord				2022		
Holy, Holy, Holy! Lord God Almighty	64	4	79			
How Great Thou Art	77	2	61			
I Love You, Lord				2068		
I Will Call upon the Lord				2002		
Jesus Shall Reign Where'er the Sun	157					
Let All Things Now Living				2008		
Let Us with a Joyful Mind				2012		
Let's Sing Unto the Lord (Cantemos al Señor)	149	49	67			
More Precious than Silver				2065		
My Life Flows On				2212		170
Now, on Land and Sea Descending	685		372			
O Crucified Redeemer	425					
Praise the Name of Jesus				2066		
Praise the Source of Faith and Learning				2004		
Psalm 19:1-6						240
Psalm 19:7-14						241
This Is My Father's World	144	47	62			71
This Is the Day the Lord Hath Made (TWENTY-FOURTH)	658					
Thy Word Is a Lamp unto My Feet	601		109			
To Know You More				2161		
We Sing of Your Glory				2011		
Wonderful Words of Life (Oh! Cantadmelas otra vez)	600	313				

1 Corinthians 1:18-25

Scripture Hymn Title	UMH	MVPC	CLUW	TFWS	SOZ	URW
All My Hope Is Firmly Grounded	132					
Ask Ye What Great Thing I Know	163					
Be Thou My Vision	451	240				180
Beneath the Cross of Jesus	297					
God of Grace and God of Glory	577	287				
God of the Sparrow God of the Whale	122	37	59			
Here Is Bread, Here Is Wine				2266		
In the Cross of Christ I Glory	295					
Jesus, Keep Me Near the Cross	301				19	
Lamb of God				2113		

Scripture Hymn Title	UMH	MVPC	CLUW	TFWS	SOZ	URW
Lift High the Cross	159	164	174			
Morning Glory, Starlit Sky	194					
O Christ, the Healer, We Have Come	265					
O How He Loves You and Me				2108		
O the Depth of Love Divine	627					
Praise the Source of Faith and Learning				2004		
Sing, My Tongue, the Glorious Battle	296					
The Head that Once Was Crowned with Thorns	326					
The Old Rugged Cross	504	142				
When I Survey the Wondrous Cross (HAMBURG)	298	138				
When I Survey the Wondrous Cross (ROCKINGHAM)	299					

John 2:13-22

Scripture Hymn Title	UMH	MVPC	CLUW	TFWS	SOZ	URW
Ah, Holy Jesus, How Hast Thou Offended	289		186			
At the Name of Jesus Every Knee Shall Bow	168					
Beneath the Cross of Jesus	297					
God Is Here	660					
God the Sculptor of the Mountains				2060		
Jesus Walked This Lonesome Valley				2112		
Jesus, Name above All Names				2071		
Lord of the Dance (I Danced in the Morning)	261	128	170			
Lord, Who Throughout These Forty Days	269	181				
O Christ, the Healer, We Have Come	265					
O Crucified Redeemer	425					
O Love, How Deep, How Broad, How High	267					
O Young and Fearless Prophet	444					
Rise, Shine, You People	187					
What Does the Lord Require	441					
What Does the Lord Require of You				2174		
What Wondrous Love Is This	292					
Wild and Lone the Prophet's Voice				2089		

March 22, 2009 (Fourth Sunday in Lent)

Liturgical Color: Purple

Scripture Hymn Title	UMH	MVPC	CLUW	TFWS	SOZ	URW
Numbers 21:4-9						
Canticle of Covenant Faithfulness	125					
Give Thanks			247	2036		
God Hath Spoken by the Prophets	108	38				
If It Had Not Been for the Lord				2053		
Immortal, Invisible, God Only Wise	103		74			
My Life Is in You, Lord				2032		
Seek the Lord Who Now Is Present	124					
Sing, My Tongue, the Glorious Battle	296					
Psalm 107:1-3, 17-22						
Amazing Grace! How Sweet the Sound	378	203	94		211	
Come, Ye Disconsolate, Where'er Ye Languish	510					
Give Thanks			247	2036		
Great Is the Lord				2022		
Guide Me, O Thou Great Jehovah	127					
Now Thank We All Our God	102					
O God Beyond All Praising				2009		
Out of the Depths I Cry to You	515					
Praise the Lord Who Reigns Above	96		124			
The First Song of Isaiah				2030		
We Are Called				2172		
We Bring the Sacrifice of Praise				2031		
Ephesians 2:1-10						
Amazing Grace! How Sweet the Sound	378	203	94		211	
Celebrate Love				2073		
Christ Beside Me				2166		

Scripture Hymn Title	UMH	MVPC	CLUW	TFWS	SOZ	URW
Come, O Thou Traveler Unknown	386					148
Come, Thou Fount of Every Blessing	400	42	127			92
Depth of Mercy! Can There Be	355		273			
Faith Is Patience in the Night				2211		
Grace Alone				2162		
Grace Greater than Our Sin	365					
Here Is Bread, Here Is Wine				2266		
Just as I Am, Without One Plea	357				208	
Let Us Plead for Faith Alone	385					
Lord God, Your Love Has Called Us Here	579					
Majesty, Worship His Majesty	176	171	204			
Marvelous Grace of Our Loving Lord	365					
O How He Loves You and Me				2108		
Rock of Ages, Cleft for Me	361	247				
Savior, Like a Shepherd Lead Us	381					
There's a Wideness in God's Mercy	121					
We Walk by Faith				2196		

John 3:14-21

Scripture Hymn Title	UMH	MVPC	CLUW	TFWS	SOZ	URW
Because He Lives	364	154	285			
Beneath the Cross of Jesus	297					
Breathe on Me, Breath of God	420					167
Canticle of Light and Darkness	205					
Celebrate Love				2073		
Christ Is the World's Light	188					
Come, Let Us with Our Lord Arise				2084		
Crown Him with Many Crowns	327	157				
Give Thanks			247	2036		
God Hath Spoken by the Prophets	108	38				
Grace Greater than Our Sin	365					
Hallelujah! What a Savior	165					
He Came Down				2085		
Help Us Accept Each Other	560		253			
How Great Thou Art	77	2	61			
I Want to Walk as a Child of the Light	206		102			
Into My Heart				2160		
Jesus, Keep Me Near the Cross	301				19	
Lead Me, Guide Me				2214		

Scripture Hymn Title	UMH	MVPC	CLUW	TFWS	SOZ	URW
Lift High the Cross	159	164	174			
Living for Jesus				2149		
Lord, I Lift Your Name on High				2088		
Lord, I Want to Be a Christian	402	215			76	
Man of Sorrows! What a Name	165					
Marvelous Grace of Our Loving Lord	365					
More Like You				2167		
Morning Glory, Starlit Sky	194					
Mothering God, You Gave Me Birth				2050		
O Holy Spirit, Root of Life				2121		79
O How He Loves You and Me				2108		
O Love Divine, What Hast Thou Done	287		185			
O Love, How Deep, How Broad, How High	267					
Of the Father's Love Begotten	184	52	66			
Rise, Shine, You People	187					

March 29, 2009 (Fifth Sunday in Lent)

Liturgical Color: Purple

Scripture Hymn Title	UMH	MVPC	CLUW	TFWS	SOZ	URW
Jeremiah 31:31-34						
Change My Heart, O God			278	2152		
Come and Fill Our Hearts				2157		378
Come, Let Us Use the Grace Divine	606					135
Give Me a Clean Heart				2133	182	
God Is So Good				2056	231	
God the Sculptor of the Mountains				2060		
Great Is Thy Faithfulness	140	30	81			
Here I Am, Lord (I, the Lord of Sea and Sky)	593	289	263			
I Want a Principle Within	410					
If Thou But Suffer God to Guide Thee	142					
Life-giving Bread				2261		
O Love that Wilt Not Let Me Go	480	255	322			
Please Enter My Heart, Hosanna				2154		
Psalm 51:1-12						
Breathe on Me, Breath of God	420					167
Change My Heart, O God			278	2152		
Depth of Mercy! Can There Be	355		273			
Fix Me, Jesus	655				122	
Forgive Us, Lord				2134		
Give Me a Clean Heart				2133	182	
Have Thine Own Way, Lord!	382	213	327			
I Want a Principle Within	410					
Jesus, Lover of My Soul	479					
Jubilate, Servite				2017		383
Just as I Am, Without One Plea	357				208	
Let Us Pray to the Lord	485					

Scripture Hymn Title	UMH	MVPC	CLUW	TFWS	SOZ	URW
O For a Heart to Praise My God	417					
Open Our Eyes				2086		
Pass Me Not, O Gentle Savior	351		271			
Please Enter My Heart, Hosanna				2154		
Sunday's Palms Are Wednesday's Ashes				2138		
Thy Holy Wings, O Savior	502					

Hebrews 5:5-10

	UMH	MVPC	CLUW	TFWS	SOZ	URW
'Tis Finished! The Messiah Dies	282		182			
Ah, Holy Jesus, How Hast Thou Offended	289		186			
At the Name of Jesus Every Knee Shall Bow	168					
Blessed Assurance, Jesus Is Mine!	369	65	287			
Blow Ye the Trumpet, Blow	379	309				
Crown Him with Many Crowns	327	157				
Hail, Thou Once Despised Jesus	325					
Humble Thyself in the Sight of the Lord				2131		
Love the Lord Your God				2168		
Make Me a Captive, Lord	421					
My Song Is Love Unknown				2083		
Nothing But the Blood	362					
O Love Divine, What Hast Thou Done	287		185			
O the Lamb, the Loving Lamb	300					
Victim Divine				2259		
What Can Wash Away My Sin	362					

John 12:20-33

	UMH	MVPC	CLUW	TFWS	SOZ	URW
A Charge to Keep I Have	413					
And Are We Yet Alive	553					
Beneath the Cross of Jesus	297					
Christ for the World We Sing	568		260			
Dear Lord, Lead Me Day by Day	411		100			
For the Healing of the Nations	428					
Glorify Thy Name				2016		
Go to Dark Gethsemane	290		187			
Hallelujah! What a Savior	165					
Healer of Our Every Ill				2213		161
Hymn of Promise (In the Bulb There Is a Flower)	707	338	392			
I Can Hear My Savior Calling	338					

Scripture Hymn Title	UMH	MVPC	CLUW	TFWS	SOZ	URW
I Have Decided to Follow Jesus				2129		
Jesus Calls Us o'er the Tumult	398		96			
Lead On, O King Eternal	580	174				
Lift High the Cross	159	164	174			
Living for Jesus				2149		
Make Me a Channel of Your Peace				2171		
Man of Sorrows! What a Name	165					
Mil Voces Para Celebrar	59					
Must Jesus Bear the Cross Alone	424					
My Faith Looks Up to Thee	452				215	
Now the Green Blade Riseth	311					
O For a Thousand Tongues to Sing	57	1	226			
O Jesus, I Have Promised	396	214				
One Bread, One Body	620	324	237			
Open Our Eyes				2086		
Rise Up, O Men of God	576					
Take Up Thy Cross, the Savior Said	415		145			
The Summons				2130		60
Together We Serve				2175		
We Would See Jesus	256		168			
Where He Leads Me	338				42	

April 5, 2009 (Palm/Passion Sunday)

Liturgical Color: Purple

Scripture Hymn Title	UMH	MVPC	CLUW	TFWS	SOZ	URW

LITURGY OF THE PALMS

Mark 11:1-11

Hymn Title	UMH	MVPC	CLUW	TFWS	SOZ	URW
All Glory, Laud, and Honor	280					
Blessed Be the Name of the Lord				2034		
Heleluyan, Heleluyan	78	39	354			405
Holy, Holy, Holy				2007		
Holy, Holy, Holy Lord				2256		
Holy, Holy, Holy! Lord God Almighty	64	4	79			
Hosanna! Hosanna!				2109		
Hosanna, Loud Hosanna, the Little Children Sang	278					
Mantos Y Palmas (Filled with Excitement)	279	136	178			
My Song Is Love Unknown				2083		
Please Enter My Heart, Hosanna				2154		
Rejoice, Ye Pure in Heart (MARION)	160		130			
Rejoice, Ye Pure in Heart (VINEYARD HAVEN)	161					
Sunday's Palms Are Wednesday's Ashes				2138		
Tell Me the Stories of Jesus	277		177			
The King of Glory Comes				2091		
This Is the Feast of Victory	638					
We Sang Our Glad Hosannas				2111		

Psalm 118:1-2, 19-29

Hymn Title	UMH	MVPC	CLUW	TFWS	SOZ	URW
All Glory, Laud, and Honor	280					
Alleluia (Celtic)				2043		
Blessed Be the Name of the Lord				2034		
By Gracious Powers So Wonderfully Sheltered	517					

Scripture Hymn Title	UMH	MVPC	CLUW	TFWS	SOZ	URW
Cares Chorus				2215		
Christ Is Made the Sure Foundation	559					
Come, Let Us with Our Lord Arise				2084		
Good Christian Friends, Rejoice	224		155			
He Has Made Me Glad				2270		
Heleluyan, Heleluyan	78	39	354			405
Holy, Holy, Holy Lord				2256		
Hosanna! Hosanna!				2109		
How Long, O Lord				2209		
Jesus Walked This Lonesome Valley				2112		
Jesus, Savior, Lord (Saranam, Saranam)	523		105			
Lead Me, Lord	473					226
Lord, Listen to Your Children				2207		
Mantos Y Palmas (Filled with Excitement)	279	136	178			
O Sacred Head, Now Wounded	286	139				
Precious Lord, Take My Hand	474		309		179	
Stand By Me	512				41	
Taste and See				2267		258
Thank You, Jesus				2081		
The King of Glory Comes				2091		
This Is the Day the Lord Hath Made (TWENTY-FOURTH)	658					
This Is the Day, This Is the Day	657					
We Sang Our Glad Hosannas				2111		
What Gift Can We Bring	87					127
When the Storms of Life Are Raging	512					
You Are Mine				2218		

LITURGY OF THE PASSION

Isaiah 50:4-9a

Come, Let Us with Our Lord Arise				2084		
Cry of My Heart				2165		
Goodness Is Stronger than Evil				2219		436
He Never Said a Mumbalin' Word	291				101	
If Thou But Suffer God to Guide Thee	142					
Lord, Speak to Me, that I May Speak	463					
Morning Glory, Starlit Sky	194					

Scripture Hymn Title	UMH	MVPC	CLUW	TFWS	SOZ	URW
Near to the Heart of God (There Is a Place of Quiet Rest)	472		324			
Nothing Can Trouble				2054		388
O Sacred Head, Now Wounded	286	139				
Open My Eyes, that I May See	454	184				
Open Our Eyes				2086		
Precious Lord, Take My Hand	474		309		179	
They Crucified My Lord	291					

Psalm 31:9-16

By Gracious Powers So Wonderfully Sheltered	517					
Cares Chorus				2215		
How Long, O Lord				2209		
Jesus Walked This Lonesome Valley				2112		
Jesus, Savior, Lord (Saranam, Saranam)	523		105			
Lead Me, Lord	473					226
Lord, Listen to Your Children				2207		
O Sacred Head, Now Wounded	286	139				
Precious Lord, Take My Hand	474		309		179	
Stand By Me	512				41	
When the Storms of Life Are Raging	512					
You Are Mine				2218		

Philippians 2:5-11

All Glory, Laud, and Honor	280					
All Hail the Power of Jesus' Name (Coronation)	154	60				
All Hail the Power of Jesus' Name (Diadem)	155					
All Praise to Thee, for Thou, O King Divine	166					
And Can It Be that I Should Gain	363	206	280			
Angels from the Realms of Glory	220					
At the Name of Jesus Every Knee Shall Bow	168					
Canticle of Christ's Obedience	167					
Christ the Lord Is Risen Today	302	152	193			
Come and See				2127		
Creator of the Stars of Night	692					218
Hail, Thou Once Despised Jesus	325					
He Is Exalted				2070		

Scripture Hymn Title	UMH	MVPC	CLUW	TFWS	SOZ	URW
He Is Lord, He Is Lord!	177	173			233	
Hosanna, Loud Hosanna, the Little Children Sang	278					
Jesus! the Name High over All	193		199			
Jesus, Name above All Names				2071		
Lord, I Lift Your Name on High				2088		
Lord, Whose Love Through Humble Service	581					204
Make Me a Servant				2176		
Mothering God, You Gave Me Birth				2050		
O How I Love Jesus (There Is a Name I Love to Hear)	170		198		36	
Praise the Name of Jesus				2066		
Precious Name	536					
Rejoice, the Lord Is King (Darwall's 148th)	715					
Rejoice, the Lord Is King (Gopsal)	716					
Rejoice, Ye Pure in Heart (Marion)	160		130			
Rejoice, Ye Pure in Heart (Vineyard Haven)	161					
Take the Name of Jesus with You	536					
The Servant Song (Brother, Sister, Let Me Serve You)				2222		117
Thou Didst Leave Thy Throne			172	2100		
We Are Singing\We Are Marching\Siyahamba				2235		
We Will Glorify the King of Kings				2087		
What Wondrous Love Is This	292					
When Morning Gilds the Skies	185		369		184	
Woke Up This Morning				2082		

Mark 14:1–15:47 or Mark 15:1-39, (40-47)

	UMH	MVPC	CLUW	TFWS	SOZ	URW
Ah, Holy Jesus, How Hast Thou Offended	289		186			
Alas! and Did My Savior Bleed (Martyrdom)	294					
Alas! and Did My Savior Bleed (Hudson)	359	202			8	
All Glory, Laud, and Honor	280					
Amen, Amen				2072		
An Outcast Among Outcasts				2104		
Become to Us the Living Bread	630					
Blessed Be the Name of the Lord				2034		
Bread of the World in Mercy Broken	624		240			

Scripture Hymn Title	UMH	MVPC	CLUW	TFWS	SOZ	URW
Broken for Me				2263		
By Gracious Powers So Wonderfully Sheltered	517					
Come, Let Us Eat	625					
Eat This Bread, Drink This Cup	628					379
For the Bread Which You Have Broken (Beng-Li)	615					
For the Bread Which You Have Broken (For the Bread)	614	235				
For Your Generous Providing						82
Go to Dark Gethsemane	290		187			
Hallelujah! We Sing Your Praises						400
Have Thine Own Way, Lord!	382	213	327			
He Never Said a Mumbalin' Word	291				101	
He Touched Me (Shackled by a Heavy Burden)	367	209	286		72	
Heleluyan, Heleluyan	78	39	354			405
Holy, Holy, Holy				2007		
Holy, Holy, Holy Lord				2256		
Holy, Holy, Holy! Lord God Almighty	64	4	79			
Hosanna! Hosanna!				2109		
Hosanna, Loud Hosanna, the Little Children Sang	278					
I Come with Joy to Meet My Lord	617					120
I Surrender All	354	225			67	
Lamb of God				2113		
Let Us Break Bread Together	618	316	236		88	
Let Us Talents and Tongues Employ						96
Life-giving Bread				2261		
Lift High the Cross	159	164	174			
Lo, He Comes with Clouds Descending	718					
Lord of the Dance (I Danced in the Morning)	261	128	170			
Lord, I Lift Your Name on High				2088		
Lord, Whose Love Through Humble Service	581					204
Lord, You Give the Great Commission	584					
Mantos Y Palmas (Filled with Excitement)	279	136	178			
Marvelous Grace of Our Loving Lord	365					
Mothering God, You Gave Me Birth				2050		

Scripture Hymn Title	UMH	MVPC	CLUW	TFWS	SOZ	URW
My Jesus, I Love Thee	172		321			
My Song Is Love Unknown				2083		
Now in This Banquet						121
Now the Silence	619					
O Love Divine, What Hast Thou Done	287		185			
O Love, How Deep, How Broad, How High	267					
O Sacred Head, Now Wounded	286	139				
O the Depth of Love Divine	627					
Please Enter My Heart, Hosanna				2154		
Rejoice, Ye Pure in Heart (MARION)	160		130			
Rejoice, Ye Pure in Heart (VINEYARD HAVEN)	161					
Sing, My Tongue, the Glorious Battle	296					
Spirit Song	347	190	91			
Stay with Me				2198		
Sunday's Palms Are Wednesday's Ashes				2138		
Take Our Bread	640		238			
Tell Me the Stories of Jesus	277		177			
The Bread of Life for All Is Broken	633					
The Hand of Heaven						124
The King of Glory Comes				2091		
They Crucified My Lord	291					
This Is My Body (Este Es Mi Cuerpo)						421
This Is the Body of Christ						420
This Is the Feast of Victory	638					
To Mock Your Reign, O Dearest Lord	285		184			
Turn Your Eyes upon Jesus	349					
We Sang Our Glad Hosannas				2111		
Were You There When They Crucified My Lord?	288	137			126	
What Wondrous Love Is This	292					
When I Survey the Wondrous Cross (HAMBURG)	298	138				
When in Our Music God Is Glorified	68		129			
Why Has God Forsaken Me?				2110		
Within the Reign of God						128
Woman in the Night	274					
Would I Have Answered When You Called				2137		

April 9, 2009 (Holy Thursday)

Liturgical Color: Purple

Scripture Hymn Title	UMH	MVPC	CLUW	TFWS	SOZ	URW
Exodus 12:1-4, (5-10), 11-14						
A Mother Lined a Basket				2189		
Deep in the Shadows of the Past				2246		
El Shaddai	123	45	77			
Go Down, Moses	448				112	
God the Sculptor of the Mountains				2060		
Guide Me, O Thou Great Jehovah	127					
He Has Made Me Glad				2270		
He Leadeth Me: O Blessed Thought	128	237				
Here, O My Lord, I See Thee	623					
In the Midst of New Dimensions				2238		
Jesus, Savior, Lord (Saranam, Saranam)	523		105			
Lead Me, Lord	473					226
Lead On, O Cloud of Presence				2234		
O Crucified Redeemer	425					
O God Beyond All Praising				2009		
O God, Our Help in Ages Past	117					200
Shepherd Me, O God				2058		
Spirit, Spirit of Gentleness				2120		
We Bring the Sacrifice of Praise				2031		
We Gather Together to Ask the Lord's Blessing	131	361				
Wellspring of Wisdom	506					173
You Satisfy the Hungry Heart	629					
Psalm 116:1-2, 12-19						
Children of the Heavenly Father	141		335			
Come, My Way, My Truth, My Life	164					

Scripture Hymn Title	UMH	MVPC	CLUW	TFWS	SOZ	URW
Come, Sinners, to the Gospel Feast *Communion*	616					
Give Thanks			247	2036		
I Love You, Lord				2068		
I Will Call upon the Lord				2002		
Jesus, Savior, Lord (Saranam, Saranam)	523		105			
More Love to Thee, O Christ	453		318			
My Tribute	99					
O Lord, Hear My Prayer				2200		390
Praise to the Lord, the Almighty	139	29	68			63
Thank You, Lord	84				228	
There Are Some Things I May Not Know				2147		
We Bring the Sacrifice of Praise				2031		
What Gift Can We Bring	87					127

1 Corinthians 11:23-26

As We Gather at Your Table				2268		
Because Thou Hast Said	635					
Bread of the World in Mercy Broken	624		240			
Broken for Me				2263		
Come, Share the Lord				2269		
Come, Sinners, to the Gospel Feast *Communion*	616					
Eat This Bread, Drink This Cup	628					379
For the Bread Which You Have Broken (Beng-Li)	615					
For the Bread Which You Have Broken (For the Bread)	614	235				
For Your Generous Providing						82
Hallelujah! We Sing Your Praises						400
Here Is Bread, Here Is Wine				2266		
Here, O Lord, Your Servants Gather	552		251			
I Come with Joy to Meet My Lord	617					120
In Remembrance of Me				2254		
In the Singing				2255		
Let Us Break Bread Together	618	316	236		88	
Let Us Talents and Tongues Employ						96
Life-giving Bread				2261		

Scripture Hymn Title	UMH	MVPC	CLUW	TFWS	SOZ	URW
Lord, You Give the Great Commission	584					
Mothering God, You Gave Me Birth				2050		
Now in This Banquet						121
Now It Is Evening				2187		
O Crucified Redeemer	425					
Take Our Bread	640		238			
The Bread of Life for All Is Broken	633					
The Church of Christ, in Every Age	589					
The Hand of Heaven						124
This Is My Body (Este Es Mi Cuerpo)						421
This Is the Body of Christ						420
Una Espiga	637	319				
Within the Reign of God						128

John 13:1-17, 31b-35

Scripture Hymn Title	UMH	MVPC	CLUW	TFWS	SOZ	URW
Ah, Holy Jesus, How Hast Thou Offended	289		186			
As We Gather at Your Table				2268		
Bind Us Together				2226		
Bread of the World in Mercy Broken	624		240			
By Gracious Powers So Wonderfully Sheltered	517					
Canticle of Love	646					
Christ, Be Our Light						114
Come Down, O Love Divine	475					
Come, Ye Disconsolate, Where'er Ye Languish	510					
Draw Us in the Spirit's Tether	632					
Father, I Adore You			225	2038		
Go to Dark Gethsemane	290		187			
God Is Here	660					
Great God, Your Love Has Called Us Here						87
He Came Down				2085		
Healer of Our Every Ill				2213		161
Jesu, Jesu, Fill Us with Your Love	432	288	179			116
Jesus, Thine All-Victorious Love	422					
Jesus' Hands Were Kind Hands	273		176			
Joy in the Morning				2284		
Let Us Be Bread				2260		

Scripture Hymn Title	UMH	MVPC	CLUW	TFWS	SOZ	URW
Live in Charity (UBI CARITAS)				2179		394
Lord God, Your Love Has Called Us Here	579					
Lord, Speak to Me, that I May Speak	463					
Lord, Whose Love Through Humble Service	581					204
Love Divine, All Loves Excelling	384					100
Make Me a Channel of Your Peace				2171		
Make Me a Servant				2176		
Make Us One				2224		
O Love Divine, What Hast Thou Done	287		185			
O Love, How Deep, How Broad, How High	267					
O Sacred Head, Now Wounded	286	139				
O Thou Who Camest from Above	501		269			
Praise with Joy the World's Creator						73
The Church of Christ, in Every Age						589
The Gift of Love (Though I May Speak with Bravest Fire)	408		341			141
The Servant Song (Brother, Sister, Let Me Serve You)				2222		117
There's a Spirit in the Air	192					
They'll Know We Are Christians by Our Love (We Are One in the Spirit)			257	2223		
Together We Serve				2175		
We Sang Our Glad Hosannas				2111		
We Will Glorify the King of Kings				2087		
Were You There When They Crucified My Lord?	288	137				126
What Wondrous Love Is This	292					
When the Church of Jesus Shuts Its Outer Door	592					
Where Charity and Love Prevail	549					
Who Is He in Yonder Stall	190					
Wounded World that Cries for Healing				2177		
You Satisfy the Hungry Heart	629					

April 10, 2009 (Good Friday)

Liturgical Color: None

Scripture Hymn Title	UMH	MVPC	CLUW	TFWS	SOZ	URW
Isaiah 52:13–53:12						
Ah, Holy Jesus, How Hast Thou Offended	289		186			
Alas! and Did My Savior Bleed (Hudson)	359	202			8	
Alas! and Did My Savior Bleed (Martyrdom)	294					
And Can It Be that I Should Gain	363	206	280			
Crown Him with Many Crowns	327	157				
Hallelujah! What a Savior	165					
He Never Said a Mumbalin' Word	291				101	
Lord, I Lift Your Name on High				2088		
Man of Sorrows! What a Name	165					
Morning Glory, Starlit Sky	194					
My Song Is Love Unknown				2083		
O How He Loves You and Me				2108		
O Sacred Head, Now Wounded	286	139				
The Strife Is O'er, the Battle Done	306					
They Crucified My Lord	291					
To Mock Your Reign, O Dearest Lord	285	184				
Victim Divine				2259		
What Wondrous Love Is This	292					
Psalm 22						
All People that on Earth Do Dwell	75	118				
Angels from the Realms of Glory	220					
By Gracious Powers So Wonderfully Sheltered	517					
Come Down, O Love Divine	475					
Give Thanks			247	2036		
Glory to God				2033		

Scripture Hymn Title	UMH	MVPC	CLUW	TFWS	SOZ	URW
God Will Take Care of You (Nunca desmayes)	130	260				
Goodness Is Stronger than Evil				2219		436
How Long, O Lord				2209		
How Majestic Is Your Name				2023		
I Want Jesus to Walk with Me	521		104		95	110
I Will Trust in the Lord	464		292		14	
I'll Praise My Maker While I've Breath	60		123			
Jesus, Tempted in the Desert				2105		
Lead Me, Lord	473					226
Let Us Plead for Faith Alone	385					
My Faith Looks Up to Thee	452				215	
Nobody Knows the Trouble I See	520				170	
O Sacred Head, Now Wounded	286	139				
O Worship the King, All-Glorious Above	73					
Out of the Depths				2136		
Out of the Depths I Cry to You	515					
Pass Me Not, O Gentle Savior	351		271			
Praise the Lord Who Reigns Above	96		124			
Praise to the Lord				2029		309
Praise, My Soul, the King of Heaven	66					75
Precious Lord, Take My Hand	474		309		179	
Remember Me, Remember Me	491		234		235	
Savior, Like a Shepherd Lead Us	381					
Taste and See				2267		258
The God of Abraham Praise	116	28				
The Lord's Prayer (WEST INDIAN)	271					
Trust and Obey (When We Walk with the Lord)	467		320			
We Sing of Your Glory				2011		
What Wondrous Love Is This	292					
When We Are Called to Sing Your Praise				2216		
Why Has God Forsaken Me?				2110		
Why Stand So Far Away, My God?				2180		
You Satisfy the Hungry Heart	629					

Hebrews 10:16-25

Blessed Assurance, Jesus Is Mine!	369	65	287			

Scripture	Hymn Title	UMH	MVPC	CLUW	TFWS	SOZ	URW
	Come, Thou Fount of Every Blessing	400	42	127			92
	I Am Thine, O Lord	419	218				
	Live in Charity (Ubi Caritas)				2179		394
	Near to the Heart of God (There Is a Place of Quiet Rest)	472		324			
	Since Jesus Came into My Heart				2140		
	Take Our Bread	640		238			
	There Is a Fountain Filled with Blood	622					
	This Is the Feast of Victory	638					
	'Tis Finished! The Messiah Dies	282		182			
	Victim Divine				2259		
	Wash, O God, Our Sons and Daughters	605					

John 18:1–19:42

Scripture	Hymn Title	UMH	MVPC	CLUW	TFWS	SOZ	URW
	'Tis Finished! The Messiah Dies	282		182			
	Ah, Holy Jesus, How Hast Thou Offended	289		186			
	Alas! and Did My Savior Bleed (Hudson)	359	202			8	
	Alas! and Did My Savior Bleed (Martyrdom)	294					
	All Hail King Jesus				2069		
	And Can It Be that I Should Gain	363	206	280			
	Awesome God				2040		
	Beneath the Cross of Jesus	297					
	Go to Dark Gethsemane	290		187			
	Hail, Thou Once Despised Jesus	325					
	Hallelujah! What a Savior	165					
	He Never Said a Mumbalin' Word	291				101	
	Here Am I				2178		
	Jesus Walked This Lonesome Valley				2112		
	Jesus, Remember Me	488	249	364			382
	Lamb of God				2113		
	Let All Mortal Flesh Keep Silence	626		150		217	
	Living for Jesus				2149		
	Lo, He Comes with Clouds Descending	718					
	Lord of the Dance (I Danced in the Morning)	261	128	170			
	Lord, I Lift Your Name on High				2088		
	Man of Sorrows! What a Name	165					
	Morning Glory, Starlit Sky	194					

Scripture Hymn Title	UMH	MVPC	CLUW	TFWS	SOZ	URW
My God, I Love Thee	470					
My Song Is Love Unknown				2083		
O Church of God, United	547		249			
O How He Loves You and Me				2108		
O Love Divine, What Hast Thou Done	287		185			
O Love, How Deep, How Broad, How High	267					
O Sacred Head, Now Wounded	286	139				
O Sing a Song of Bethlehem	179					
O the Lamb, the Loving Lamb	300					
Rejoice, the Lord Is King (DARWALL'S 148TH)	715					
Rejoice, the Lord Is King (GOPSAL)	716					
Rock of Ages, Cleft for Me	361	247				
Sent Out in Jesus' Name				2184		
Sing, My Tongue, the Glorious Battle	296					
Stay with Me				2198		
Stay with Us				2199		115
Swiftly Pass the Clouds of Glory				2102		
The Bread of Life for All Is Broken	633					
The Old Rugged Cross	504	142				
They Crucified My Lord	291					
They Crucified My Savior	316		189			
Thou Didst Leave Thy Throne			172	2100		
To Mock Your Reign, O Dearest Lord	285		184			
Victim Divine				2259		
We Sang Our Glad Hosannas				2111		
We've a Story to Tell to the Nations	569					
Were You There When They Crucified My Lord?	288	137			126	
What Feast of Love						119
What Wondrous Love Is This	292					
When I Survey the Wondrous Cross (HAMBURG)	298	138				
When I Survey the Wondrous Cross (ROCKINGHAM)	299					
When Jesus Wept	2106					
Who Is He in Yonder Stall	190					
Why Has God Forsaken Me?				2110		
Why Stand So Far Away, My God?				2180		
Woman in the Night	274					

April 12, 2009 (Easter Day)

Liturgical Color: White

Scripture Hymn Title	UMH	MVPC	CLUW	TFWS	SOZ	URW
Acts 10:34-43						
At the Font We Start Our Journey				2114		
Christ Jesus Lay in Death's Strong Bands	319					
Come, Be Baptized				2252		
Come, Ye Faithful, Raise the Strain	315					
For the Healing of the Nations	428					
God Hath Spoken by the Prophets	108	38				
Hail Thee, Festival Day	324					
Holy				2019		
Holy God, We Praise Thy Name	79		80			
I Come with Joy to Meet My Lord	617					120
Lord of the Dance (I Danced in the Morning)	261	128	170			
O Sing a Song of Bethlehem	179					
Oh, I Know the Lord's Laid His Hands on Me				2139		
The Strife Is O'er, the Battle Done	306					
This Is My Song	437					
Water, River, Spirit, Grace				2253		
We Meet You, O Christ	257					
We Would See Jesus	256		168			
When Jesus Came to Jordan	252	125				
Who Is He in Yonder Stall	190					
You Alone Are Holy				2077		
Psalm 118:1-2, 14-24						
All Glory, Laud, and Honor	280					
Alleluia	186		355			
Alleluia (CELTIC)				2043		

Scripture Hymn Title	UMH	MVPC	CLUW	TFWS	SOZ	URW
Alleluia (HONDURAS)				2078		
Come, Let Us with Our Lord Arise				2084		
Good Christian Friends, Rejoice	224		155			
He Has Made Me Glad				2270		
Heleluyan, Heleluyan	78	39	354			405
In Thee Is Gladness	169					
Let Us with a Joyful Mind				2012		
My Tribute	99					
Stand Up and Bless the Lord	662		128			
Taste and See				2267		258
Thank You, Jesus				2081		
The Day of Resurrection	303		188			
This Is the Day the Lord Hath Made (TWENTY-FOURTH)	658					
This Is the Day, This Is the Day	657					
What Gift Can We Bring	87					127
You Alone Are Holy				2077		

1 Corinthians 15:1-11

Scripture Hymn Title	UMH	MVPC	CLUW	TFWS	SOZ	URW
Alleluia	186		355			
Amazing Grace! How Sweet the Sound	378	203	94		211	
Amen, Amen				2072		
And Can It Be that I Should Gain	363	206	280			
At the Font We Start Our Journey				2114		
Christ Has Risen				2115		
Christ Is Risen! Shout Hosanna!	307					
Christ Is Risen, Christ Is Living	313					
Christ Jesus Lay in Death's Strong Bands	319					
Christ the Lord Is Risen				2116		
Christ the Lord Is Risen Today	302	152	193			
Come, Be Baptized				2252		
Come, Thou Fount of Every Blessing	400	42	127			92
Come, Ye Faithful, Raise the Strain	315					
Cristo Vive, Fuera el Llanto	313					
Easter People, Raise Your Voices	304				6	
For the Healing of the Nations	428					
God Hath Spoken by the Prophets	108	38				
Grace Alone				2162		

Scripture Hymn Title	UMH	MVPC	CLUW	TFWS	SOZ	URW
Hail Thee, Festival Day	324					
He Is Lord, He Is Lord!	177	173			233	
He Lives	310	149			30	
Holy				2019		
Holy God, We Praise Thy Name	79		80			
I Come with Joy to Meet My Lord	617					120
Lord of the Dance (I Danced in the Morning)	261	128	170			
Lord, I Lift Your Name on High				2088		
Now the Green Blade Riseth	311					
O How I Love Jesus (There Is a Name I Love to Hear)	170		198		36	
O Sing a Song of Bethlehem	179					
O Sons and Daughters, Let Us Sing	317					
Oh, I Know the Lord's Laid His Hands on Me				2139		
Shout to the Lord				2074		
Sing with All the Saints in Glory	702		382			
Something Beautiful, Something Good	394		303			
The Day of Resurrection	303		188			
The Strife Is O'er, the Battle Done	306					
The Voice of God Is Calling	436		139			
There Is a Fountain Filled with Blood	622					
This Is My Song	437					
Water, River, Spirit, Grace				2253		
We Meet You, O Christ	257					
We Would See Jesus	256		168			
When Jesus Came to Jordan	252	125				
Who Is He in Yonder Stall	190					
You Alone Are Holy				2077		

John 20:1-18 (or Mark 16:1-8)

Scripture Hymn Title	UMH	MVPC	CLUW	TFWS	SOZ	URW
A Blessing (I Pray that Christ May Come)						112
Alleluia	186		355			
Alleluia (Honduras)				2078		
As Man and Woman We Were Made	642					
Camina, Pueblo de Dios (Walk On, O People of God)	305	151				
Christ Has Risen				2115		
Christ Is Alive! Let Christians Sing	318		190			

Scripture Hymn Title	UMH	MVPC	CLUW	TFWS	SOZ	URW
Christ Is Risen! Shout Hosanna!	307					
Christ Is Risen, Christ Is Living	313					
Christ the Lord Is Risen				2116		
Christ the Lord Is Risen Today	302	152	193			
Cristo Vive, Fuera el Llanto	313					
Crown Him with Many Crowns	327	157				
Easter People, Raise Your Voices	304					6
Good Christian Friends, Rejoice	224		155			
Hail the Day that Sees Him Rise	312	158				
Hark! the Herald Angels Sing	240	101				
He Is Lord, He Is Lord!	177	173			233	
He Lives	310	149			30	
He Rose	316				168	
In the Garden	314	242	296		44	
Lord, I Lift Your Name on High				2088		
My Faith Looks Up to Thee	452				215	
Now the Green Blade Riseth	311					
O Mary, Don't You Weep, Don't You Mourn	134				153	
O Sons and Daughters, Let Us Sing	317					
On the Day of Resurrection	309					
Sing Alleluia to the Lord				2258		404
The Day of Resurrection	303		188			
The First One Ever, Oh, Ever to Know	276					
The Strife Is O'er, the Battle Done	306					
They Crucified My Savior	316		189			
Thine Be the Glory, Risen, Conquering Son	308	155	194			
Up from the Grave He Arose (Low in the Grave He Lay)	322	147	192			
Walk with Me				2242		118
We Humans Build to Frame a Life						168
We Sang Our Glad Hosannas				2111		
What Gift Can We Bring	87					127
Woman in the Night	274					

April 19, 2009 (Second Sunday of Easter)

Liturgical Color: White

Scripture Hymn Title	UMH	MVPC	CLUW	TFWS	SOZ	URW
Acts 4:32-35						
All Praise to Our Redeeming Lord	554					
Because He Lives	364	154	285			
Blest Be the Tie that Binds	557	347				
Camina, Pueblo de Dios (Walk On, O People of God)	305	151				
Canticle of Light and Darkness	205					
Christ Is the World's Light	188					
Close to Thee	407				7	
Draw Us in the Spirit's Tether	632					
Grace Alone				2162		
Hail, Thou Once Despised Jesus	325					
Here, O Lord, Your Servants Gather	552		251			
Here, O My Lord, I See Thee	623					
I Want to Walk as a Child of the Light	206		102			
Jesus, Lord, We Look to Thee	562					
Jesus, Lover of My Soul	479					
Jesus, United by Thy Grace	561					
Just as I Am, Without One Plea	357				208	
Lead Me, Guide Me				2214		
Light of the World				2204		
Living for Jesus				2149		
Lord, We Come to Ask Your Blessing				2230		
Make Me a Channel of Your Peace				2171		
Mil Voces Para Celebrar	59					
My Hope Is Built on Nothing Less	368	261				
O For a Thousand Tongues to Sing	57	1	226			
O Splendor of God's Glory Bright	679					211

Scripture Hymn Title	UMH	MVPC	CLUW	TFWS	SOZ	URW
Shine, Jesus, Shine			264	2173		
They'll Know We Are Christians by Our Love (We Are One in the Spirit)			257	2223		
To God Be the Glory, Great Things He Hath Done!	98	169	78			
Trust and Obey (When We Walk with the Lord)	467		320			
We All Are One in Mission				2243		
We Are Called				2172		
Where Charity and Love Prevail	549					

Psalm 133

Scripture Hymn Title	UMH	MVPC	CLUW	TFWS	SOZ	URW
All Praise to Our Redeeming Lord	554					
And Are We Yet Alive	553					
Bind Us Together				2226		
Blest Be the Tie that Binds	557	347				
Help Us Accept Each Other	560		253			
How Can We Name a Love	111					
How Good It Is (Psalm 133)						335
In Christ There Is No East or West	548				65	
In Unity We Lift Our Song				2221		
Live in Charity (Ubi Caritas)				2179		394
Make Us One				2224		
O Day of God, Draw Nigh	730					
O Look and Wonder				2231		
Our Parent, by Whose Name	447					
Shalom Chaverim	667	351	362			
The Gift of Love (Though I May Speak with Bravest Fire)	408		341			141
Weave						57
When Cain Killed Abel				2135		
Where Charity and Love Prevail	549					

1 John 1:1–2:2

Scripture Hymn Title	UMH	MVPC	CLUW	TFWS	SOZ	URW
Because He Lives	364	154	285			
Camina, Pueblo de Dios (Walk On, O People of God)	305	151				
Canticle of Light and Darkness	205					
Christ Is the World's Light	188					

Scripture Hymn Title	UMH	MVPC	CLUW	TFWS	SOZ	URW
Close to Thee	407				7	
Draw Us in the Spirit's Tether	632					
Hail, Thou Once Despised Jesus	325					
Here, O My Lord, I See Thee	623					
I Want to Walk as a Child of the Light	206		102			
Jesus, Lover of My Soul	479					
Just as I Am, Without One Plea	357				208	
Lead Me, Guide Me				2214		
Light of the World				2204		
Living for Jesus				2149		
Make Me a Channel of Your Peace				2171		
Mil Voces Para Celebrar	59					
My Hope Is Built on Nothing Less	368	261				
O For a Thousand Tongues to Sing	57	1	226			
O Splendor of God's Glory Bright	679					211
Shine, Jesus, Shine			264	2173		
To God Be the Glory, Great Things He Hath Done!	98	169	78			
Trust and Obey (When We Walk with the Lord)	467		320			
We Are Called				2172		

John 20:19-31

Scripture Hymn Title	UMH	MVPC	CLUW	TFWS	SOZ	URW
Blessed Jesus, at Thy Word	596		108			
Breathe on Me, Breath of God	420					167
Christ Has Risen				2115		
Christ Is Alive! Let Christians Sing	318		190			
Christ Is Risen! Shout Hosanna!	307					
Christ Jesus Lay in Death's Strong Bands	319					
Christian People, Raise Your Song	636					
Dona Nobis Pacem	376	360	142			443
Easter People, Raise Your Voices	304				6	
Enemy of Apathy						165
Faith Is Patience in the Night				2211		
Forgive Our Sins as We Forgive	390					
God, How Can We Forgive				2169		
Hail the Day that Sees Him Rise	312	158				
He Is Lord, He Is Lord!	177	173			233	

Scripture Hymn Title	UMH	MVPC	CLUW	TFWS	SOZ	URW
He Lives	310	149			30	
Here Is Bread, Here Is Wine				2266		
Holy Spirit, Come, Confirm Us	331		217			
Holy Spirit, Truth Divine	465					
In the Singing				2255		
Let It Breathe on Me	503				224	
Lo, He Comes with Clouds Descending	718					
Love Divine, All Loves Excelling	384					100
Now It Is Evening				2187		
O Breath of Life, Come Sweeping through Us	543					
O Sons and Daughters, Let Us Sing	317					
Of All the Spirit's Gifts to Me	336					
Open Our Eyes				2086		
Please Enter My Heart, Hosanna				2154		
Savior, Again to Thy Dear Name	663	349				
Send Me, Lord	497		331			
Spirit of God				2117		
Spirit of God, Descend upon My Heart	500					
Spirit, Working in Creation						150
Surely the Presence of the Lord Is in This Place	328	344	215			
The Day of Resurrection	303		188			
The First One Ever, Oh, Ever to Know	276					
Thine Be the Glory, Risen, Conquering Son	308	155	194			
'Tis So Sweet to Trust in Jesus	462					
Turn Your Eyes upon Jesus	349					
Walk with Me				2242		118
We Walk by Faith				2196		
When Our Confidence Is Shaken	505					
Where Charity and Love Prevail	549					
Where the Spirit of the Lord Is				2119		
Without Seeing You				2206		
Womb of Life				2046		

April 26, 2009 (Third Sunday of Easter)

Liturgical Color: White

Scripture Hymn Title	UMH	MVPC	CLUW	TFWS	SOZ	URW
Acts 3:12-19						
And Can It Be that I Should Gain	363	206	280			
Christ Has Risen				2115		
Come, Sinners, to the Gospel Feast *Communion*	616					
Come, Sinners, to the Gospel Feast *Invitation*	339		88			
Come, Ye Sinners, Poor and Needy	340					
He Lives	310	149			30	
Healer of Our Every Ill				2213		161
My Song Is Love Unknown				2083		
Now the Green Blade Riseth	311					
Psalm 4						
Cares Chorus				2215		
Children of the Heavenly Father	141		335			
God Has Smiled on Me					196	
If Thou But Suffer God to Guide Thee	142					
Lead Me, Guide Me				2214		
Lead Me, Lord	473					226
Lord of All Hopefulness				2197		179
My Soul Is at Rest						387
Please Enter My Heart, Hosanna				2154		
Precious Lord, Take My Hand	474	309			179	
We Bring the Sacrifice of Praise				2031		
You Are Mine				2218		

Scripture Hymn Title	UMH	MVPC	CLUW	TFWS	SOZ	URW
1 John 3:1-7						
Amazing Grace! How Sweet the Sound	378	203	94		211	
And Can It Be that I Should Gain	363	206	280			
Baptized in Water				2248		
Celebrate Love				2073		
Change My Heart, O God			278	2152		
Children of the Heavenly Father	141		335			
Christ Has Risen				2115		
Come, Sinners, to the Gospel Feast *Communion*	616					
Come, Sinners, to the Gospel Feast *Invitation*	339		88			
Come, We that Love the Lord (Marching to Zion)	733				3	13
Come, We that Love the Lord (St. Thomas)	732					
Come, Ye Sinners, Poor and Needy	340					
Cry of My Heart				2165		
God, Whose Love Is Reigning o'er Us	100		73			74
He Came Down				2085		
He Lives	310	149			30	
Healer of Our Every Ill				2213		161
Holy, Holy				2039		
I Want a Principle Within	410					
Jesus, the Very Thought of Thee	175					
Jesus, Thine All-Victorious Love	422					
Lord, I Want to Be a Christian	402	215			76	
Lord, Listen to Your Children				2207		
Love Divine, All Loves Excelling	384					100
My Song Is Love Unknown				2083		
Now the Green Blade Riseth	311					
O How He Loves You and Me				2108		
O Love that Wilt Not Let Me Go	480	255	322			
O Love, How Deep, How Broad, How High	267					
O World of God						147
Praise, My Soul, the King of Heaven	66					75
Sing with All the Saints in Glory	702		382			
Take Time to Be Holy	395					

Scripture Hymn Title	UMH	MVPC	CLUW	TFWS	SOZ	URW
The Strife Is O'er, the Battle Done	306					
There Are Some Things I May Not Know	2147					
Water Has Held Us						187
Your Love, O God, Has Called Us Here	647					

Luke 24:36b-48

	UMH	MVPC	CLUW	TFWS	SOZ	URW
Alleluia, Alleluia! Give Thanks to the Risen Lord	162					
Camina, Pueblo de Dios (Walk On, O People of God)	305	151				
Christ for the World We Sing	568		260			
Christ Is Risen! Shout Hosanna!	307					
Christ the Lord Is Risen Today	302	152	193			
Come, Let Us with Our Lord Arise				2084		
Come, Ye Faithful, Raise the Strain	315					
Go Ye, Go Ye into the World				2239		
Hail the Day that Sees Him Rise	312	158				
Hail, Thou Once Despised Jesus	325					
He Is Lord, He Is Lord!	177	173			233	
He Lives	310	149				30
O Sons and Daughters, Let Us Sing	317					
Surely the Presence of the Lord Is in This Place	328	344	215			
The Day of Resurrection	303		188			
The Strife Is O'er, the Battle Done	306					
Thine Be the Glory, Risen, Conquering Son	308	155	194			

May 3, 2009 (Fourth Sunday of Easter)

Liturgical Color: White

Scripture Hymn Title	UMH	MVPC	CLUW	TFWS	SOZ	URW
Acts 4:5-12						
Am I a Soldier of the Cross	511					
At the Name of Jesus Every Knee Shall Bow	168					
Christ Is Made the Sure Foundation	559					
God of Grace and God of Glory	577	287				
Grace Alone				2162		
He Is Lord, He Is Lord!	177	173			233	
Jesus, Name above All Names				2071		
Majesty, Worship His Majesty	176	171	204			
My Hope Is Built on Nothing Less	368	261				
O For a Thousand Tongues to Sing	57	1	226			
The Church's One Foundation	545	269	255			
We Are God's People				2220		
We've a Story to Tell to the Nations	569					
You Alone Are Holy				2077		
Psalm 23						
Close to Thee	407				7	
Come and Find the Quiet Center				2128		
Come Away from Rush and Hurry						202
Gentle Shepherd (Psalm 23)						246
Give Me the Faith Which Can Remove	650					
Go Now in Peace	665		363			
God Is My Rock/El Señor Es Mi Fuerza (Psalm 62)						278
Goodness Is Stronger than Evil				2219		436
He Leadeth Me: O Blessed Thought	128	237				
His Name Is Wonderful	174	172	203			

Scripture Hymn Title	UMH	MVPC	CLUW	TFWS	SOZ	URW
I Was There to Hear Your Borning Cry				2051		
If It Had Not Been for the Lord				2053		
Jesus Walked This Lonesome Valley				2112		
Lamb of God				2113		
Lead Me, Guide Me				2214		
Lord, Dismiss Us with Thy Blessing	671					
My Shepherd, You Supply My Need (Psalm 23)						244
Nothing Can Trouble				2054		388
Now It Is Evening				2187		
O Thou, in Whose Presence My Soul Takes Delight	518					
Precious Lord, Take My Hand	474		309		179	
Psalm 23 (King James Version)	137					
Savior, Like a Shepherd Lead Us	381					
Send Me, Lord	497		331			
Shepherd Me, O God				2058		
Since Jesus Came into My Heart				2140		
The King of Love My Shepherd Is	138					
The Lord's My Shepherd, I'll Not Want	136	115				
Thou My Everlasting Portion	407					
Without Seeing You				2206		
You Are Mine				2218		
You Are My Hiding Place				2055		
Your Goodness and Love (Psalm 23)						245

1 John 3:16-24

Abide with Me; Fast Falls the Eventide	700					
Am I a Soldier of the Cross	511					
At the Name of Jesus Every Knee Shall Bow	168					
Bind Us Together				2226		
Blest Be the Dear Uniting Love	566		254			
Breathe on Me, Breath of God	420					167
Canticle of Love	646					
Christ Is Made the Sure Foundation	559					
Father, I Adore You			225	2038		
God of Grace and God of Glory	577	287				
Grace Alone				2162		

Scripture Hymn Title	UMH	MVPC	CLUW	TFWS	SOZ	URW
He Is Lord, He Is Lord!	177	173			233	
Healer of Our Every Ill				2213		161
Here Am I				2178		
I Come with Joy to Meet My Lord	617					120
Jesu, Jesu, Fill Us with Your Love	432	288	179			116
Jesus, Draw Me Close				2159		
Jesus, Name above All Names				2071		
Lead On, O King Eternal	580	174				
Living for Jesus				2149		
Lord, Whose Love Through Humble Service	581					204
Majesty, Worship His Majesty	176	171	204			
My Hope Is Built on Nothing Less	368	261				
O For a Thousand Tongues to Sing	57	1	226			
People Need the Lord				2244		
The Church's One Foundation	545	269	255			
The Gift of Love (Though I May Speak with Bravest Fire)	408		341			141
The King of Love My Shepherd Is	138					
They'll Know We Are Christians by Our Love (We Are One in the Spirit)			257	2223		
We Are God's People				2220		
We've a Story to Tell to the Nations	569					
When We Are Living (Pues Si Vivimos)	356	337	310			175
Where Charity and Love Prevail	549					
Within the Day-to-Day				2245		
You Alone Are Holy				2077		

John 10:11-18

Abide with Me; Fast Falls the Eventide	700					
Ah, Holy Jesus, How Hast Thou Offended	289		186			
At the Name of Jesus Every Knee Shall Bow	168					
Give Me the Faith Which Can Remove	650					
Go in Peace, Walk in Love						444
God Be with You till We Meet Again (GOD BE WITH YOU)	672		347		37	
God Be with You till We Meet Again (RANDOLPH)	673					
Good Christian Friends, Rejoice	224		155			

Scripture Hymn Title	UMH	MVPC	CLUW	TFWS	SOZ	URW
His Name Is Wonderful	174	172	203			
How Like a Gentle Spirit	115		216			
I Am Thine, O Lord	419	218				
Now Praise the Hidden God of Love				2027		
O For a Thousand Tongues to Sing	57	1	226			
O Thou, in Whose Presence My Soul Takes Delight	518					
Psalm 23 (King James Version)	137					
Savior, Like a Shepherd Lead Us	381					
Shepherd Me, O God				2058		
Source and Sovereign, Rock and Cloud	113					
The King of Love My Shepherd Is	138					
The Lord's My Shepherd, I'll Not Want	136		115			
We Are One in Christ Jesus				2229		
You Satisfy the Hungry Heart	629					

May 10, 2009 (Fifth Sunday of Easter)

Liturgical Color: White

Scripture Hymn Title	UMH	MVPC	CLUW	TFWS	SOZ	URW
Acts 8:26-40						
Baptized in Water				2248		
Christ for the World We Sing	568	260				
Come, Holy Ghost, Our Hearts Inspire	603	218				
Come, Let Us Use the Grace Divine	606					135
Enemy of Apathy						165
Go, Make of All Disciples	571					261
I've Just Come from the Fountain				2250		
Lord, I Lift Your Name on High				2088		
People Need the Lord				2244		
We Know that Christ Is Raised	610	231				
We Were Baptized in Christ Jesus				2251		
We've a Story to Tell to the Nations	569					
Psalm 22:25-31						
All People that on Earth Do Dwell	75	118				
Angels from the Realms of Glory	220					
How Majestic Is Your Name				2023		
O Worship the King, All-Glorious Above	73					
Praise to the Lord				2029		309
Praise, My Soul, the King of Heaven	66					75
1 John 4:7-21						
As Man and Woman We Were Made	642					
Baptized in Water				2248		
Canticle of Love	646					
Christ for the World We Sing	568	260				
Christ Is the World's Light	188					
Come Now, O Prince of Peace (O-so-so)			148	2232		415

Scripture Hymn Title	UMH	MVPC	CLUW	TFWS	SOZ	URW
Come, and Let Us Sweetly Join	699					
Come, Holy Ghost, Our Hearts Inspire	603	218				
Come, Let Us Use the Grace Divine	606					135
Enemy of Apathy						165
Father, I Adore You			225	2038		
Go, Make of All Disciples	571	261				
God Is So Good				2056	231	
God of Many Names	105					
He Came Down				2085		
Help Us Accept Each Other	560	253				
I Sought the Lord, and Afterward I Knew	341					
I've Just Come from the Fountain				2250		
Jesus, Joy of Our Desiring	644	344				
Jesus, Thine All-Victorious Love	422					
Live in Charity (Ubi Caritas)				2179		394
Lord, I Lift Your Name on High				2088		
Love Came Down at Christmas	242					
Love Divine, All Loves Excelling	384					100
My God, I Love Thee	470					
My Jesus, I Love Thee	172	321				
Near to the Heart of God (There Is a Place of Quiet Rest)	472	324				
O How He Loves You and Me				2108		
O How I Love Jesus (There Is a Name I Love to Hear)	170	198		36		
O Love, How Deep, How Broad, How High	267					
O Perfect Love, All Human Thought Transcending	645					
People Need the Lord				2244		
The Gift of Love (Though I May Speak with Bravest Fire)	408	341				141
They'll Know We Are Christians by Our Love (We Are One in the Spirit)			257	2223		
We Are God's People				2220		
We Know that Christ Is Raised	610	231				
We Were Baptized in Christ Jesus				2251		
We've a Story to Tell to the Nations	569					
What Wondrous Love Is This	292					

Scripture Hymn Title	UMH	MVPC	CLUW	TFWS	SOZ	URW
Where Charity and Love Prevail	549					
Your Love, O God, Has Called Us Here	647					

John 15:1-8

Scripture Hymn Title	UMH	MVPC	CLUW	TFWS	SOZ	URW
Christ Is Made the Sure Foundation	559					
Christ Loves the Church	590					
Forth in Thy Name, O Lord, I Go	438					
God the Sculptor of the Mountains				2060		
How Can We Name a Love	111					
How Like a Gentle Spirit	115	216				
I Need Thee Every Hour	397					
Like the Murmur of the Dove's Song	544					
Live in Charity (Ubi Caritas)				2179		394
Lord, Be Glorified				2150		
Lord, We Come to Ask Your Blessing				2230		
Mothering God, You Gave Me Birth				2050		
O Blessed Spring				2076		
Sent Forth By God's Blessing	664	366				
Soon and Very Soon	706	385			198	
Source and Sovereign, Rock and Cloud	113					
The Summons				2130		60
There's a Spirit in the Air	192					

May 17, 2009 (Sixth Sunday of Easter)

Liturgical Color: White

Scripture Hymn Title	UMH	MVPC	CLUW	TFWS	SOZ	URW
Acts 10:44-48						
At the Font We Start Our Journey				2114		
Blest Be the Tie that Binds	557	347				
Come Down, O Love Divine	475					
Cry of My Heart				2165		
Filled with the Spirit's Power	537					
For the Healing of the Nations	428					
Give Me the Faith Which Can Remove	650					
Goodness Is Stronger than Evil				2219		436
Help Us Accept Each Other	560	253				
Here, O Lord, Your Servants Gather	552	251				
I Know Whom I Have Believed (I Know Not Why God's Wondrous Grace)	714	290				
I Want a Principle Within	410					
I Was There to Hear Your Borning Cry				2051		
In Christ There Is No East or West	548				65	
I've Just Come from the Fountain				2250		
Jesus, Draw Me Close				2159		
Let Us Plead for Faith Alone	385					
Light of the World				2204		
Make Me a Captive, Lord	421					
O Holy Spirit, Root of Life				2121		79
Our Parent, by Whose Name	447					
Praise and Thanksgiving Be to God	604	230				
See How Great a Flame Aspires	541	248				
Since Jesus Came into My Heart				2140		
Spirit of Faith, Come Down	332	219				
Victory in Jesus	370	92				

Scripture Hymn Title	UMH	MVPC	CLUW	TFWS	SOZ	URW
We Know that Christ Is Raised	610		231			
We Sang Our Glad Hosannas				2111		
We Were Baptized in Christ Jesus				2251		
Weary of All Trumpeting	442					
Where Charity and Love Prevail	549					

Psalm 98

Scripture Hymn Title	UMH	MVPC	CLUW	TFWS	SOZ	URW
All Creatures of Our God and King	62	22				
Camina, Pueblo de Dios (Walk On, O People of God)	305	151				
Children of the Heavenly Father	141		335			
Clap Your Hands				2028		
Joy to the World, the Lord Is Come!	246	100	161			
Let All the World in Every Corner Sing	93					
Let's Sing Unto the Lord (Cantemos al Señor)	149	49	67			
Praise the Lord Who Reigns Above	96		124			
Praise the Lord with the Sound of Trumpet				2020		
Praise to the Lord, the Almighty	139	29	68			63
Shout to the Lord				2074		
Sing a New Song (Psalm 98)						296
Sing a New Song to the Lord				2045		
The Head that Once Was Crowned with Thorns	326					
The Strife Is O'er, the Battle Done	306					
The Trees of the Field				2279		
When in Our Music God Is Glorified	68		129			

1 John 5:1-6

Scripture Hymn Title	UMH	MVPC	CLUW	TFWS	SOZ	URW
Cry of My Heart				2165		
For the Healing of the Nations	428					
Give Me the Faith Which Can Remove	650					
Goodness Is Stronger than Evil				2219		436
I Know Whom I Have Believed (I Know Not Why God's Wondrous Grace)	714		290			
I Want a Principle Within	410					
I Was There to Hear Your Borning Cry				2051		
Jesus, Draw Me Close				2159		
Let Us Plead for Faith Alone	385					

Scripture Hymn Title	UMH	MVPC	CLUW	TFWS	SOZ	URW
Light of the World				2204		
Make Me a Captive, Lord	421					
Our Parent, by Whose Name	447					
Since Jesus Came into My Heart				2140		
Victory in Jesus	370		92			
We Know that Christ Is Raised	610		231			
We Sang Our Glad Hosannas				2111		
Weary of All Trumpeting	442					
Where Charity and Love Prevail	549					

John 15:9-17

Scripture Hymn Title	UMH	MVPC	CLUW	TFWS	SOZ	URW
As Man and Woman We Were Made	642					
Bind Us Together				2226		
Blessed Quietness				2142	206	
Blest Be the Tie that Binds	557	347				
Canticle of Love	646					
Christ Is Made the Sure Foundation	559					
Come Down, O Love Divine	475					
Come, Christians, Join to Sing	158					
Crown Him with Many Crowns	327	157				
Filled with the Spirit's Power	537					
He Came Down				2085		
Healer of Our Every Ill				2213		161
Help Us Accept Each Other	560		253			
Here, O Lord, Your Servants Gather	552		251			
I Come with Joy to Meet My Lord	617					120
In Christ There Is No East or West	548				65	
Jesu, Jesu, Fill Us with Your Love	432	288	179			116
Jesus Calls Us Here to Meet Him						56
Jesus Is All the World to Me	469	234			216	
Jesus Our Friend and Brother	659					
Let Us Be Bread				2260		
Love Divine, All Loves Excelling	384					100
Loving Spirit				2123		203
Make Us One				2224		
My Song Is Love Unknown				2083		
Now It Is Evening				2187		
O How He Loves You and Me				2108		

Scripture Hymn Title	UMH	MVPC	CLUW	TFWS	SOZ	URW
O Jesus, My King and My Sovereign (Jesús Es Mi Rey Soberano)	180	54				
The Gift of Love (Though I May Speak with Bravest Fire)	408		341			141
They'll Know We Are Christians by Our Love (We Are One in the Spirit)			257	2223		
We Are Called				2172		
What a Friend We Have in Jesus	526	257	333			
Where Charity and Love Prevail	549					

May 21, 2009 (Ascension of the Lord) (May also be used Sunday, May 24, 2009)

Liturgical Color: White

Scripture Hymn Title	UMH	MVPC	CLUW	TFWS	SOZ	URW
Acts 1:1-11						
All Hail the Power of Jesus' Name (Coronation)	154	60				
All Hail the Power of Jesus' Name (Diadem)	155					
Alleluia, Alleluia! Give Thanks to the Risen Lord	162					
Ask Ye What Great Thing I Know	163					
At the Font We Start Our Journey				2114		
At the Name of Jesus Every Knee Shall Bow	168					
Baptized in Water				2248		
Camina, Pueblo de Dios (Walk On, O People of God)	305	151				
Christ Has Risen				2115		
Christ Is Made the Sure Foundation	559					
Christ Is Risen, Christ Is Living	313					
Christ Is the World's Light	188					
Christ Jesus Lay in Death's Strong Bands	319					
Christ the Lord Is Risen				2116		
Christ the Lord Is Risen Today	302	152	193			
Christ, Whose Glory Fills the Skies	173		281			
Come Down, O Love Divine	475					
Come, Holy Ghost, Our Hearts Inspire	603		218			
Come, Share the Lord				2269		
Come, Ye Faithful, Raise the Strain	315					
Cristo Vive, Fuera el Llanto	313					
Crown Him with Many Crowns	327	157				
For All the Saints, Who from Their Labors Rest	711	384	388			

Scripture Hymn Title	UMH	MVPC	CLUW	TFWS	SOZ	URW
Glory to God in the Highest				2276		
Hail the Day that Sees Him Rise	312	158				
Hail Thee, Festival Day	324					
Hail, Thou Once Despised Jesus	325					
He Is Exalted				2070		
He Lives	310	149			30	
His Name Is Wonderful	174	172	203			
Holy God, We Praise Thy Name	79		80			
Holy Spirit, Come to Us				2118		395
Hope of the World	178					
I'll Fly Away				2282	183	
Jesus Shall Reign Where'er the Sun	157					
Jesus, Name above All Names				2071		
Kum Ba Yah, My Lord	494		332		139	
Life-giving Bread				2261		
Like the Murmur of the Dove's Song	544					
Lord, I Lift Your Name on High				2088		
Loving Spirit				2123		203
My Hope Is Built on Nothing Less	368	261				
Nothing Can Trouble				2054		388
Open My Eyes, that I May See	454	184				
Open Our Eyes				2086		
See How Great a Flame Aspires	541		248			
Spirit of Faith, Come Down	332		219			
Spirit of God				2117		
The Fragrance of Christ				2205		
The Head that Once Was Crowned with Thorns	326					
The Trees of the Field				2279		
There Are Some Things I May Not Know				2147		
Thine Be the Glory, Risen, Conquering Son	308	155	194			
Up from the Grave He Arose (Low in the Grave He Lay)	322	147	192			
We Are God's People				2220		
We Will Glorify the King of Kings				2087		
When in Our Music God Is Glorified	68		129			
Wonder of Wonders				2247		
You Are Worthy				2063		

Scripture Hymn Title	UMH	MVPC	CLUW	TFWS	SOZ	URW
Psalm 47						
All People that on Earth Do Dwell	75		118			
Awesome God				2040		
Christ Is the World's Light	188					
Clap Your Hands				2028		
Crown Him with Many Crowns	327	157				
Glory to God in the Highest				2276		
Hail, Thou Once Despised Jesus	325					
He Is Exalted				2070		
Jesus Shall Reign Where'er the Sun	157					
Laudate Dominum (Sing Praise and Bless the Lord)						384
Let All the World in Every Corner Sing	93					
Lord, I Lift Your Name on High				2088		
Majesty, Worship His Majesty	176	171	204			
Praise the Lord Who Reigns Above	96		124			
Shout to the Lord				2074		
Sing Praise to God Who Reigns Above	126		60		70	
The Head that Once Was Crowned with Thorns	326					
The Trees of the Field				2279		
Thine Be the Glory, Risen, Conquering Son	308	155	194			
We Are Singing\We Are Marching\Siyahamba				2235		
We, Thy People, Praise Thee	67		72			
What a Mighty God We Serve				2021		
Ephesians 1:15-23						
All Hail the Power of Jesus' Name (Coronation)	154	60				
All Hail the Power of Jesus' Name (Diadem)	155					
Christ Is Made the Sure Foundation	559					
Come, Share the Lord				2269		
Crown Him with Many Crowns	327	157				
For All the Saints, Who from Their Labors Rest	711	384	388			
Glory to God in the Highest				2276		
Hail, Thou Once Despised Jesus	325					
His Name Is Wonderful	174	172	203			

Scripture Hymn Title	UMH	MVPC	CLUW	TFWS	SOZ	URW
Holy God, We Praise Thy Name	79		80			
Hope of the World	178					
Jesus Shall Reign Where'er the Sun	157					
Jesus, Name above All Names				2071		
Life-giving Bread				2261		
My Hope Is Built on Nothing Less	368	261				
Nothing Can Trouble				2054		388
Open My Eyes, that I May See	454	184				
Open Our Eyes				2086		
The Fragrance of Christ				2205		
The Head that Once Was Crowned with Thorns	326					
The Trees of the Field				2279		
There Are Some Things I May Not Know				2147		
We Are God's People				2220		
When in Our Music God Is Glorified	68		129			
You Are Worthy				2063		

Luke 24:44-53

Alleluia (Honduras)				2078		
Alleluia, Alleluia! Give Thanks to the Risen Lord	162					
As We Gather at Your Table				2268		
Ascension (Prayer)	323					
Ask Ye What Great Thing I Know	163					
At the Font We Start Our Journey				2114		
Camina, Pueblo de Dios (Walk On, O People of God)	305	151				
Christ Has Risen				2115		
Christ Is Risen! Shout Hosanna!	307					
Christ Is Risen, Christ Is Living	313					
Christ Jesus Lay in Death's Strong Bands	319					
Christ the Lord Is Risen				2116		
Christ the Lord Is Risen Today	302	152	193			
Come, Let Us with Our Lord Arise				2084		
Come, Ye Faithful, Raise the Strain	315					
Cristo Vive, Fuera el Llanto	313					
Crown Him with Many Crowns	327	157				

Scripture	Hymn Title	UMH	MVPC	CLUW	TFWS	SOZ	URW
	Go Ye, Go Ye into the World				2239		
	Hail the Day that Sees Him Rise	312	158				
	Hail Thee, Festival Day	324					
	Hail, Thou Once Despised Jesus	325					
	He Is Exalted				2070		
	He Lives	310	149			30	
	I'll Fly Away				2282	183	
	Jesus Shall Reign Where'er the Sun	157					
	Lord God, Almighty				2006		
	Majesty, Worship His Majesty	176	171	204			
	Rejoice, the Lord Is King (DARWALL'S 148TH)	715					
	Rejoice, the Lord Is King (GOPSAL)	716					
	Sent Forth By God's Blessing	664		366			
	Sent Out in Jesus' Name				2184		
	Spirit of God				2117		
	Stay with Us				2199		115
	The Head that Once Was Crowned with Thorns	326					
	The Spirit Sends Us Forth to Serve				2241		
	Who Is He in Yonder Stall	190					
	Wonder of Wonders				2247		
	You Alone Are Holy				2077		

May 24, 2009 (Seventh Sunday of Easter) (Or use Ascension readings for May 21, 2009)

Liturgical Color: White

Scripture Hymn Title	UMH	MVPC	CLUW	TFWS	SOZ	URW
Acts 1:15-17, 21-26						
Forward Through the Ages	555					
Give Me the Faith Which Can Remove	650					
God the Spirit, Guide and Guardian	648					
Hail, Thou Once Despised Jesus	325					
To God Be the Glory, Great Things He Hath Done!	98	169	78			
We Believe in One True God	85					
We've a Story to Tell to the Nations	569					
Psalm 1						
A Charge to Keep I Have	413					
All My Hope Is Firmly Grounded	132					
Blessed Jesus, at Thy Word	596		108			
Guide My Feet				2208		
Happy Are They (Psalm 1)						223
Happy Is the One (Psalm 1)						224
He Has Made Me Glad				2270		
If Thou But Suffer God to Guide Thee	142					
Lead Me, Guide Me				2214		
Love the Lord Your God				2168		
My Life Is in You, Lord				2032		
Nothing Can Trouble				2054		388
O Blessed Spring				2076		
O Word of God Incarnate	598					
On Eagle's Wings	143		83			
Praise the Name of Jesus				2066		

Scripture Hymn Title	UMH	MVPC	CLUW	TFWS	SOZ	URW
Praise the Source of Faith and Learning				2004		
Righteous and Just Is the Word of Our Lord (La Palabra Del Señor Es Recta)	107					
Seek the Lord Who Now Is Present	124					
The First Song of Isaiah				2030		
The Lone, Wild Bird				2052		
Through It All	507		279			
Thy Word Is a Lamp unto My Feet	601		109			

1 John 5:9-13

Scripture Hymn Title	UMH	MVPC	CLUW	TFWS	SOZ	URW
Hail, Thou Once Despised Jesus	325					
To God Be the Glory, Great Things He Hath Done!	98	169	78			
We Believe in One True God	85					

John 17:6-19

Scripture Hymn Title	UMH	MVPC	CLUW	TFWS	SOZ	URW
A Charge to Keep I Have	413					
Be Still, My Soul	534		307			
Beams of Heaven as I Go	524				10	
Break Thou the Bread of Life	599					
By Gracious Powers So Wonderfully Sheltered	517					
Hail, Thou Once Despised Jesus	325					
How Firm a Foundation	529	256				
Lift Every Voice and Sing	519				32	
Lord, Be Glorified				2150		
O Jesus, I Have Promised	396	214				
Send Me, Lord	497		331			
To God Be the Glory, Great Things He Hath Done!	98	169	78			
We Believe in One True God	85					
We'll Understand It Better By and By	525	317			55	

May 31, 2009 (Day of Pentecost)

Liturgical Color: Red

Scripture Hymn Title	UMH	MVPC	CLUW	TFWS	SOZ	URW
Acts 2:1-21						
As a Fire Is Meant for Burning				2237		
At the Name of Jesus Every Knee Shall Bow	168					
Christ Loves the Church	590					
Come Down, O Love Divine	475					
Come, Holy Ghost, Our Souls Inspire	651					
Come, Holy Spirit				2125		
Come, O Holy Spirit, Come				2124		
Come, Share the Lord				2269		
Deep in the Shadows of the Past				2246		
Enemy of Apathy						165
Eternal Father, Strong to Save				2191		
Filled with the Spirit's Power	537					
For All the Saints				2283		
Gather Us In				2236		54
God of Grace and God of Glory	577	287				
Hail Thee, Festival Day	324					
Healer of Our Every Ill				2213		161
Here, O Lord, Your Servants Gather	552		251			
Holy Ground				2272		
Holy Spirit, Come to Us				2118		395
Holy Spirit, Come, Confirm Us	331		217			
Holy Spirit, Truth Divine	465					
Holy Spirit, Wind of Heaven						66
Holy, Holy				2039		
I Love Thy Kingdom, Lord	540					
I Will Call upon the Lord				2002		

Scripture	Hymn Title	UMH	MVPC	CLUW	TFWS	SOZ	URW
	In the Midst of New Dimensions				2238		
	Jesus, Thine All-Victorious Love	422					
	Like the Murmur of the Dove's Song	544					
	Loving Spirit				2123		203
	Mothering God, You Gave Me Birth				2050		
	My Hope Is Built on Nothing Less	368	261				
	Now Praise the Hidden God of Love				2027		
	Now Thank We All Our God	102					
	O Breath of Life, Come Sweeping through Us	543					
	O Church of God, United	547		249			
	O Holy One						214
	O Spirit of the Living God	539					
	Of All the Spirit's Gifts to Me	336					
	Open Our Eyes				2086		
	See How Great a Flame Aspires	541		248			
	She Comes Sailing on the Wind				2122		
	Spirit of Faith, Come Down	332		219			
	Spirit of God				2117		
	Spirit of God, Descend upon My Heart	500					
	Spirit of the Living God, Fall Afresh on Me	393	177	214		226	
	Spirit Song	347	190	91			
	Spirit, Now Live in Me						164
	Spirit, Spirit of Gentleness				2120		
	Surely the Presence of the Lord Is in This Place	328	344	215			
	Sweet, Sweet Spirit	334	186	220			
	The Church's One Foundation	545	269	255			
	The Spirit Sends Us Forth to Serve				2241		
	This Is My Body (Este Es Mi Cuerpo)						421
	We Are the Church	558		252			
	Where the Spirit of the Lord Is				2119		
	Wind Who Makes All Winds that Blow	538					
	You Alone Are Holy				2077		

Psalm 104:24-34, 35b

Scripture	Hymn Title	UMH	MVPC	CLUW	TFWS	SOZ	URW
	All Creatures of Our God and King	62	22				
	Bless the Lord				2013		377
	Breathe on Me, Breath of God	420					167

Scripture Hymn Title	UMH	MVPC	CLUW	TFWS	SOZ	URW
God of the Sparrow God of the Whale	122	37	59			
Holy, Holy, Holy! Lord God Almighty	64	4	79			
I Sing Praises to Your Name				2037		
Immortal, Invisible, God Only Wise	103		74			
Many and Great, O God, Are Thy Things	148	50	71			232
O Worship the King, All-Glorious Above	73					
Praise Our God Above				2061		
This Is My Father's World	144	47	62			71
What a Mighty God We Serve				2021		
Wind Who Makes All Winds that Blow	538					

Romans 8:22-27

Scripture Hymn Title	UMH	MVPC	CLUW	TFWS	SOZ	URW
Blessed Jesus, at Thy Word	596		108			
Canticle of Prayer	406					
Come, Holy Ghost, Our Souls Inspire	651					
Come, O Holy Spirit, Come				2124		
Creation Sings! Each Plant and Tree						86
Cry of My Heart				2165		
Every Time I Feel the Spirit	404		213		121	
Jesus, Thine All-Victorious Love	422					
Like the Murmur of the Dove's Song	544					
My Hope Is Built on Nothing Less	368	261				
O For a Heart to Praise My God	417					
O Holy Spirit, Root of Life				2121		79
Spirit of the Living God, Fall Afresh on Me	393	177	214		226	
Wind Who Makes All Winds that Blow	538					

John 15:26-27; 16:4b-15

Scripture Hymn Title	UMH	MVPC	CLUW	TFWS	SOZ	URW
Come Down, O Love Divine	475					
Come, Holy Ghost, Our Souls Inspire	651					
Come, Holy Spirit				2125		
Come, Thou Almighty King	61	11				
Creator of the Earth and Skies	450					
Daw-Kee, Aim Daw-Tsi-Taw	330					
Healer of Our Every Ill				2213		161
I Know Whom I Have Believed (I Know Not Why God's Wondrous Grace)	714		290			
Kum Ba Yah, My Lord	494		332		139	
O God in Heaven, Grant to Thy Children	119		227			

Scripture Hymn Title	UMH	MVPC	CLUW	TFWS	SOZ	URW
O Spirit of the Living God	539					
O Thou Who This Mysterious Bread	613					
Open My Eyes, that I May See	454	184				
Spirit of Faith, Come Down	332		219			
Spirit of the Living God, Fall Afresh on Me	393	177	214		226	
Spirit Song	347	190	91			
Surely the Presence of the Lord Is in This Place	328	344	215			
Where the Spirit of the Lord Is				2119		
Wind Who Makes All Winds that Blow	538					

June 7, 2009 (Trinity Sunday) (First Sunday after Pentecost)

Liturgical Color: White

Scripture Hymn Title	UMH	MVPC	CLUW	TFWS	SOZ	URW
Isaiah 6:1-8						
Bless His Holy Name				2015		
Canticle of the Holy Trinity	80					
Communion Setting				2257		
Day Is Dying in the West	687					
Here I Am, Lord (I, the Lord of Sea and Sky)	593	289	263			
Holy				2019		
Holy God, We Praise Thy Name	79		80			
Holy Ground				2272		
Holy, Holy				2039		
Holy, Holy, Holy				2007		
Holy, Holy, Holy (Sanctus from a Groaning Creation)						154
Holy, Holy, Holy Lord				2256		
Holy, Holy, Holy! Lord God Almighty	64	4	79			
Honor and Praise				2018		
I'm Gonna Live So God Can Use Me				2153		
Let All Mortal Flesh Keep Silence	626		150		217	
Maker, in Whom We Live	88					
Psalm 24 (King James Version)	212					
¡Santo! ¡Santo! ¡Santo!	65					
Send Me, Lord	497		331			
Stand Up and Bless the Lord	662		128			
The God of Abraham Praise	116	28				
The Voice of God Is Calling	436		139			
This Is the Feast of Victory	638					

Scripture Hymn Title	UMH	MVPC	CLUW	TFWS	SOZ	URW
We Believe in One True God	85					
Whom Shall I Send?	582					
Ye Watchers and Ye Holy Ones	90					

Psalm 29

Scripture Hymn Title	UMH	MVPC	CLUW	TFWS	SOZ	URW
Awesome God				2040		
Blessed Be the Name of the Lord				2034		
Father, I Adore You			225	2038		
Gloria, Gloria	72		353			380
Glory to God				2033		
God of the Sparrow God of the Whale	122	37	59			
God Weeps				2048		
Great Is the Lord				2022		
Holy				2019		
Holy, Holy, Holy Lord				2256		
Holy, Holy, Holy! Lord God Almighty	64	4	79			
I Sing the Almighty Power of God	152		65			
I'll Praise My Maker While I've Breath	60		123			
Let All Things Now Living				2008		
Many and Great, O God, Are Thy Things	148	50	71			232
O Worship the King, All-Glorious Above	73					
Praise and Thanksgiving Be to God	604		230			
Praise to the Lord, the Almighty	139	29	68			63
Shout to the Lord				2074		
Source and Sovereign, Rock and Cloud	113					
We Sing of Your Glory				2011		
You Alone Are Holy				2077		

Romans 8:12-17

Scripture Hymn Title	UMH	MVPC	CLUW	TFWS	SOZ	URW
Baptized in Water				2248		
Come, Let Us with Our Lord Arise				2084		
Daw-Kee, Aim Daw-Tsi-Taw	330					
Every Time I Feel the Spirit	404		213		121	
Gather Us In				2236	54	
Holy, Holy				2039		
How Can We Sinners Know	372		288			
I'm Goin'a Sing When the Spirit Says Sing	333		223		81	
In Christ There Is No East or West	548				65	

Scripture Hymn Title	UMH	MVPC	CLUW	TFWS	SOZ	URW
O How He Loves You and Me				2108		
O Thou Who Camest from Above	501		269			
O World of God						147
Spirit of God, Descend upon My Heart	500					
Spirit of the Living God, Fall Afresh on Me	393	177	214		226	
They'll Know We Are Christians by Our Love (We Are One in the Spirit)			257	2223		
Thou Hidden Love of God	414					
Womb of Life				2046		

John 3:1-17

Baptized in Water				2248		
Beneath the Cross of Jesus	297					
Blessed Assurance, Jesus Is Mine!	369	65	287			
Canticle of Covenant Faithfulness	125					
Christ Is the World's Light	188					
Crown Him with Many Crowns	327	157				
Freely, Freely (God Forgave My Sin)	389		258			
Give Thanks			247	2036		
Hallelujah! What a Savior	165					
He Came Down				2085		
How Great Thou Art	77	2	61			
I Know Whom I Have Believed (I Know Not Why God's Wondrous Grace)	714		290			
I Was There to Hear Your Borning Cry				2051		
If Thou But Suffer God to Guide Thee	142					
Jesus, Keep Me Near the Cross	301					19
Lift High the Cross	159	164	174			
Like the Murmur of the Dove's Song	544					
Lord, I Lift Your Name on High				2088		
Man of Sorrows! What a Name	165					
Morning Glory, Starlit Sky	194					
Mothering God, You Gave Me Birth				2050		
My Tribute	99					
O Love Divine, What Hast Thou Done	287		185			
O Love, How Deep, How Broad, How High	267					
Of the Father's Love Begotten	184	52	66			
Shout to the Lord				2074		

Scripture Hymn Title	UMH	MVPC	CLUW	TFWS SOZ	URW
Spirit of the Living God, Fall Afresh on Me	393	177	214	226	
The Church's One Foundation	545	269	255		
This Is a Day of New Beginnings	383	208	311		
This Is the Spirit's Entry Now	608				
To God Be the Glory, Great Things He Hath Done!	98	169	78		
Wash, O God, Our Sons and Daughters	605				
Water, River, Spirit, Grace				2253	
We Are God's People				2220	
We Know that Christ Is Raised	610		231		
We've a Story to Tell to the Nations	569				
What Wondrous Love Is This	292				

June 14, 2009 (Second Sunday after Pentecost)

Liturgical Color: Green

Scripture Hymn Title	UMH	MVPC	CLUW	TFWS	SOZ	URW
1 Samuel 15:34–16:13						
A Charge to Keep I Have	413					
God of Grace and God of Glory	577	287				
God of Love and God of Power	578					
Hail to the Lord's Anointed	203	81				
He Leadeth Me: O Blessed Thought	128	237				
Humble Thyself in the Sight of the Lord				2131		
Immortal, Invisible, God Only Wise	103		74			
Lead On, O Cloud of Presence				2234		
Loving Spirit				2123		203
Open My Eyes, that I May See	454	184				
Precious Lord, Take My Hand	474		309		179	
Send Me, Lord	497		331			
The Summons				2130		60
Thou My Everlasting Portion	407					
Whom Shall I Send?	582					
Psalm 20 or Psalm 72 (UMH 795)						
God of the Ages	698	377				
O God in Heaven, Grant to Thy Children	119		227			
Rejoice, Ye Pure in Heart (MARION)	160		130			
Rejoice, Ye Pure in Heart (VINEYARD HAVEN)	161					
We Gather Together to Ask the Lord's Blessing	131	361				
2 Corinthians 5:6-10, (11-13), 14-17						
Change My Heart, O God			278	2152		
Christ for the World We Sing	568		260			
Faith, While Trees Are Still in Blossom	508		97			
I Am Thine, O Lord	419	218				

Scripture Hymn Title	UMH	MVPC	CLUW	TFWS	SOZ	URW
I'll Fly Away				2282	183	
In Thee Is Gladness	169					
Jesus, Draw Me Close				2159		
Just a Closer Walk with Thee				2158	46	
Love Divine, All Loves Excelling	384					100
Make Me a Captive, Lord	421					
My Song Is Love Unknown				2083		
O Come and Dwell in Me	388					
Sanctuary				2164		
The Church's One Foundation	546					
The Church's One Foundation	545	269	255			
This Is a Day of New Beginnings	383	208	311			
We Are God's People				2220		
We Know that Christ Is Raised	610		231			
We Walk by Faith				2196		
When from Bondage We Are Summoned						153
When We Are Living (Pues Si Vivimos)	356	337	310			175
Womb of Life				2046		

Mark 4:26-34

Scripture Hymn Title	UMH	MVPC	CLUW	TFWS	SOZ	URW
Bring Forth the Kingdom				2190		
Come, Ye Thankful People, Come	694		241			
Faith Is Patience in the Night				2211		
God the Sculptor of the Mountains				2060		
Hymn of Promise (In the Bulb There Is a Flower)	707	338	392			
I Love Thy Kingdom, Lord	540					
Lead On, O Cloud of Presence				2234		
Rejoice, the Lord Is King (DARWALL'S 148TH)	715					
Rejoice, the Lord Is King (GOPSAL)	716					
Sois la Semilla (You Are the Seed)	583	291				
The Care the Eagle Gives Her Young	118		302			199
The Day Thou Gavest, Lord, Is Ended	690					
The Kingdom of God Is Like a Grain of Mustard Seed	275					
Thou Hidden Love of God	414					
We Walk by Faith				2196		

June 21, 2009 (Third Sunday after Pentecost)

Liturgical Color: Green

Scripture Hymn Title	UMH	MVPC	CLUW	TFWS	SOZ	URW
1 Samuel 17:(1a, 4-11, 19-23) 32-49						
A Mighty Fortress Is Our God	110	25				271
God of Grace and God of Glory	577	287				
Guide My Feet				2208		
How Firm a Foundation	529	256				
If It Had Not Been for the Lord				2053		
If Thou But Suffer God to Guide Thee	142					
Jesus, Savior, Lord (Saranam, Saranam)	523		105			
Lead Me, Lord	473					226
Lift Every Voice and Sing	519				32	
Make Me a Servant				2176		
O God, Our Help in Ages Past	117					200
Praise to the Lord, the Almighty	139	29	68			63
Soldiers of Christ, Arise	513					
Psalm 9:9-20						
A Mighty Fortress Is Our God	110	25				271
Awesome God				2040		
Eternal Father, Strong to Save				2191		
God of Grace and God of Glory	577	287				
If It Had Not Been for the Lord				2053		
Righteous and Just Is the Word of Our Lord (La Palabra Del Señor Es Recta)	107					
Sing Praise to God Who Reigns Above	126		60			70
Someone Asked the Question				2144		
The First Song of Isaiah				2030		
We Gather Together to Ask the Lord's Blessing	131	361				

Scripture Hymn Title	UMH	MVPC	CLUW	TFWS	SOZ	URW
We Sing to You, O God				2001		293
You Are My Hiding Place				2055		

2 Corinthians 6:1-13

Come, Ye Disconsolate, Where'er Ye Languish	510					
Creator of the Earth and Skies	450					
Holy Spirit, Truth Divine	465					
I Love Thy Kingdom, Lord	540					
In the Singing				2255		
In Thee Is Gladness	169					
It Is Well with My Soul (When Peace, Like a River, Attendeth My Way)	377	250	304		20	
Lift Every Voice and Sing	519				32	
O Day of God, Draw Nigh	730					
O For a Heart to Praise My God	417					
Sanctuary				2164		
Spirit of God, Descend upon My Heart	500					
Stand Up, Stand Up for Jesus	514					
There Are Some Things I May Not Know				2147		
We Are God's People				2220		
We Walk by Faith				2196		
Ye Servants of God, Your Master Proclaim	181					

Mark 4:35-41

A Mighty Fortress Is Our God	110	25				271
Awesome God				2040		
Be Still and Know that I Am God				2057		409
Be Still, My Soul	534		307			
Blessed Quietness				2142	206	
Eternal Father, Strong to Save				2191		
Faith Is Patience in the Night				2211		
Give to the Winds Thy Fears	129		282			
God of the Sparrow God of the Whale	122	37	59			
It Is Well with My Soul (When Peace, Like a River, Attendeth My Way)	377	250	304		20	
Jesus, Lover of My Soul	479					
Jesus, Priceless Treasure	532					
Jesus, Savior, Pilot Me	509				49	

Scripture Hymn Title	UMH	MVPC	CLUW	TFWS	SOZ	URW
Lonely the Boat, Sailing at Sea	476					
My Life Flows On				2212		170
O Jesus, I Have Promised	396	214				
Stand By Me	512				41	
Tell Me the Stories of Jesus	277		177			
When the Storms of Life Are Raging	512					
Your Song of Love						149

June 28, 2009 (Fourth Sunday after Pentecost)

Liturgical Color: Green

Scripture Hymn Title	UMH	MVPC	CLUW	TFWS	SOZ	URW
2 Samuel 1:1, 17-27						
Abide with Me; Fast Falls the Eventide	700					
Canticle of Remembrance	652					
Come, Let Us Join Our Friends Above	709		387			
Dear Lord, for All in Pain	458					
Joy Comes with the Dawn				2210		
O God, Our Help in Ages Past	117					200
Out of the Depths				2136		
Out of the Depths I Cry to You	515					
Precious Lord, Take My Hand	474		309		179	
Rejoice in God's Saints	708					
When We Are Called to Sing Your Praise				2216		
Psalm 130						
Abide with Me; Fast Falls the Eventide	700					
Be Still, My Soul	534		307			
Canticle of Redemption	516					
Cares Chorus				2215		
Come and Find the Quiet Center				2128		
Dear Lord, for All in Pain	458					
Not So in Haste, My Heart	455					
O Lord, Hear My Prayer				2200		390
Out of the Depths				2136		
Out of the Depths I Cry to You	515					
Out of the Direst Depths (Psalm 130)						328
People Need the Lord				2244		
Precious Lord, Take My Hand	474		309		179	
Why Has God Forsaken Me?				2110		

Scripture Hymn Title	UMH	MVPC	CLUW	TFWS	SOZ	URW

2 Corinthians 8:7-15

Scripture Hymn Title	UMH	MVPC	CLUW	TFWS	SOZ	URW
All Praise to Our Redeeming Lord	554					
As a Fire Is Meant for Burning				2237		
Give Thanks			247	2036		
He Became Poor						431
He Who Began a Good Work in You				2163		
Lord, Whose Love Through Humble Service	581					204
Morning Glory, Starlit Sky	194					
Once in Royal David's City	250		159			
Take My Life, and Let It Be Consecrated	399		312			
The Church of Christ, in Every Age	589					
The Spirit Sends Us Forth to Serve				2241		
There's a Spirit in the Air	192					
When the Church of Jesus Shuts Its Outer Door	592					
When the Poor Ones (Cuando El Pobre)	434	301	138			
Where Cross the Crowded Ways of Life	427	296				

Mark 5:21-43

Scripture Hymn Title	UMH	MVPC	CLUW	TFWS	SOZ	URW
An Outcast Among Outcasts				2104		
Canticle of Covenant Faithfulness	125					
Change My Heart, O God			278	2152		
Children of the Heavenly Father	141		335			
Come, Ye Disconsolate, Where'er Ye Languish	510					
Dear Lord, for All in Pain	458					
He Touched Me (Shackled by a Heavy Burden)	367	209	286		72	
Heal Me, Hands of Jesus	262					
Heal Us, Emmanuel, Hear Our Prayer	266		328			
Healer of Our Every Ill				2213		161
Here Is Bread, Here Is Wine				2266		
His Name Is Wonderful	174	172	203			
Jesus' Hands Were Kind Hands	273		176			
Let Us Plead for Faith Alone	385					
Mil Voces Para Celebrar	59					
O Christ, the Healer, We Have Come	265					

Scripture Hymn Title	UMH	MVPC	CLUW	TFWS	SOZ	URW
O For a Thousand Tongues to Sing	57	1	226			
O Lord, You're Beautiful				2064		
Oh, I Know the Lord's Laid His Hands on Me				2139		
Open Our Eyes				2086		
People Need the Lord				2244		
Precious Lord, Take My Hand	474		309		179	
Something Beautiful, Something Good	394		303			
When Jesus the Healer Passed Through Galilee	263		171			
When the Poor Ones (Cuando El Pobre)	434	301	138			
Where Cross the Crowded Ways of Life	427	296				
Woman in the Night	274					

July 5, 2009 (Fifth Sunday after Pentecost)

Liturgical Color: Green

Scripture Hymn Title	UMH	MVPC	CLUW	TFWS	SOZ	URW
2 Samuel 5:1-5, 9-10						
All My Hope Is Firmly Grounded	132					
Children of the Heavenly Father	141		335			
Come, We that Love the Lord (MARCHING TO ZION)	733				3	139
Forward Through the Ages	555					
He Leadeth Me: O Blessed Thought	128	237				
I Want to Walk as a Child of the Light	206		102			
If It Had Not Been for the Lord				2053		
O Thou, in Whose Presence My Soul Takes Delight	518					
On Eagle's Wings	143		83			
Praise to the Lord, the Almighty	139	29	68			63
What a Mighty God We Serve				2021		
Psalm 48						
Come, We that Love the Lord (MARCHING TO ZION)	733				3	139
Come, We that Love the Lord (ST. THOMAS)	732					
Glorious Things of Thee Are Spoken	731		256			
Great Is the Lord				2022		
Guide My Feet				2208		
He Leadeth Me: O Blessed Thought	128	237				
How Great Thou Art	77	2	61			
I Sing Praises to Your Name				2037		
I Will Call upon the Lord				2002		
Maker, in Whom We Live	88					
O God, Our Help in Ages Past	117					200
Praise to the Lord, the Almighty	139	29	68			63

Scripture Hymn Title	UMH	MVPC	CLUW	TFWS	SOZ	URW
Shout to the Lord				2074		
The Day Thou Gavest, Lord, Is Ended	690					
The God of Abraham Praise	116	28				
We Sing of Your Glory				2011		

2 Corinthians 12:2-10

Scripture Hymn Title	UMH	MVPC	CLUW	TFWS	SOZ	URW
Amazing Grace! How Sweet the Sound	378	203	94		211	
Be Still, My Soul	534		307			
Beams of Heaven as I Go	524				10	
By Gracious Powers So Wonderfully Sheltered	517					
Come, Thou Fount of Every Blessing	400	42	127			92
Come, Ye Sinners, Poor and Needy	340					
Faith Is Patience in the Night				2211		
Give Thanks			247	2036		
Grace Greater than Our Sin	365					
Guide My Feet				2208		
How Firm a Foundation	529	256				
If Thou But Suffer God to Guide Thee	142					
I've Been 'Buked					143	
Living for Jesus				2149		
Maker, in Whom We Live	88					
Marvelous Grace of Our Loving Lord	365					
Nobody Knows the Trouble I See	520				170	
O Love that Wilt Not Let Me Go	480	255	322			
O Thou, in Whose Presence My Soul Takes Delight	518					
Soldiers of Christ, Arise	513					
Through It All	507	279				
When Our Confidence Is Shaken	505					
You Are Mine				2218		
You Are My Hiding Place				2055		

Mark 6:1-13

Scripture Hymn Title	UMH	MVPC	CLUW	TFWS	SOZ	URW
Awesome God				2040		
Christ for the World We Sing	568	260				
Dear Lord, for All in Pain	458					
Guide My Feet				2208		
Healer of Our Every Ill				2213	161	

Scripture Hymn Title	UMH	MVPC	CLUW	TFWS	SOZ	URW
How Shall They Hear the Word of God	649					
Let Us Be Bread				2260		
Living for Jesus				2149		
Lord of All Hopefulness				2197		179
Lord, You Give the Great Commission	584					
O Zion, Haste	573					
Open My Eyes, that I May See	454	184				
Send Me, Lord	497		331			
Sent Forth By God's Blessing	664		366			
Sent Out in Jesus' Name				2184		
Sing of Mary, Pure and Lowly	272					
Spirit of God, Descend upon My Heart	500					
The Church of Christ, in Every Age	589					
The Spirit Sends Us Forth to Serve				2241		
The Summons				2130		60
'Tis So Sweet to Trust in Jesus	462					
We Meet You, O Christ	257					
We've a Story to Tell to the Nations	569					
When Jesus the Healer Passed Through Galilee	263	171				
Whom Shall I Send?	582					
Ye Servants of God, Your Master Proclaim	181					

July 12, 2009 (Sixth Sunday after Pentecost)

Liturgical Color: Green

Scripture Hymn Title	UMH	MVPC	CLUW	TFWS	SOZ	URW
2 Samuel 6:1-5, 12b-19						
El Shaddai	123	45	77			
From All that Dwell Below the Skies	101		126			
Holy Ground				2272		
Let All the World in Every Corner Sing	93					
Let's Sing Unto the Lord (Cantemos al Señor)	149	49	67			
Praise the Lord Who Reigns Above	96		124			
Praise the Lord with the Sound of Trumpet				2020		
Praise Ye the Lord				2010		372
Stand Up and Bless the Lord	662		128			
What Gift Can We Bring	87					127
When in Our Music God Is Glorified	68		129			
Psalm 24						
All Glory, Laud, and Honor	280					
All People that on Earth Do Dwell	75		118			
Change My Heart, O God			278	2152		
Christ the Lord Is Risen				2116		
Come, Thou Almighty King	61	11				
For All the Saints, Who from Their Labors Rest	711	384	388			
Hail the Day that Sees Him Rise	312	158				
He Has Made Me Glad				2270		
Holy Ground				2272		
Honor and Praise				2018		
I Sing a Song of the Saints of God	712					
Let's Sing Unto the Lord (Cantemos al Señor)	149	49	67			

Scripture	Hymn Title	UMH	MVPC	CLUW	TFWS	SOZ	URW
	Lift Up Your Heads, Ye Mighty Gates	213					
	Many and Great, O God, Are Thy Things	148	50	71			232
	My Gratitude Now Accept, O Lord				2044		
	Psalm 24 (King James Version)	212					
	The King of Glory Comes				2091		
	They Shall Receive a Blessing					209	
	This Is My Father's World	144	47	62			71
	Thou Art Worthy				2041		
	What Gift Can We Bring	87					127

Ephesians 1:3-14

Scripture	Hymn Title	UMH	MVPC	CLUW	TFWS	SOZ	URW
	Amazing Grace! How Sweet the Sound	378	203	94		211	
	Baptized in Water				2248		
	Blessed Assurance, Jesus Is Mine!	369	65	287			
	Child of Blessing, Child of Promise	611		232			
	Children of the Heavenly Father	141		335			
	Come, Thou Fount of Every Blessing	400	42	127			92
	Father, We Thank You (Albright)	563					
	Father, We Thank You (Rendez À Dieu)	565					
	Forward Through the Ages	555					
	Glory to God in the Highest				2276		
	Grace Greater than Our Sin	365					
	Hail, Thou Once Despised Jesus	325					
	He Who Began a Good Work in You				2163		
	Holy Spirit, Truth Divine	465					
	Holy, Holy				2039		
	I'm Gonna Live So God Can Use Me				2153		
	It Is Well with My Soul (When Peace, Like a River, Attendeth My Way)	377	250	304		20	
	Jesus Our Friend and Brother	659					
	Lord, Have Mercy	482					
	Loving Spirit				2123		203
	Morning Glory, Starlit Sky	194					
	My Tribute	99					
	Nothing But the Blood	362					
	There Are Some Things I May Not Know				2147		
	There Is a Fountain Filled with Blood	622					
	There's a Wideness in God's Mercy	121					

Scripture Hymn Title	UMH	MVPC	CLUW	TFWS	SOZ	URW
Victory in Jesus	370		92			
We Are God's People				2220		
What Can Wash Away My Sin	362					

Mark 6:14-29

Scripture Hymn Title	UMH	MVPC	CLUW	TFWS	SOZ	URW
Am I a Soldier of the Cross	511					
Be Still, My Soul	534		307			
Christ the Victorious, Give to Your Servants	653		380			
Faith of Our Fathers	710	385				
For All the Saints				2283		
For All the Saints, Who from Their Labors Rest	711	384	388			
God Hath Spoken by the Prophets	108	38				
Rejoice in God's Saints	708					
Sing with All the Saints in Glory	702		382			
We'll Understand It Better By and By	525	317			55	
Wild and Lone the Prophet's Voice				2089		

July 19, 2009 (Seventh Sunday after Pentecost)

Liturgical Color: Green

Scripture Hymn Title	UMH	MVPC	CLUW	TFWS	SOZ	URW
2 Samuel 7:1-14a						
All My Hope Is Firmly Grounded	132					
Bless His Holy Name				2015		
Blessed Be the God of Israel	209					12
Children of the Heavenly Father	141		335			
El Shaddai	123	45	77			
God Will Take Care of You (Nunca desmayes)	130	260				
Hail to the Lord's Anointed	203	81				
How Like a Gentle Spirit	115		216			
I Love Thy Kingdom, Lord	540					
If It Had Not Been for the Lord				2053		
It Came upon the Midnight Clear	218	90				
Jesus Shall Reign Where'er the Sun	157					
O Come, O Come, Emmanuel	211	80				
On Eagle's Wings	143		83			
See How Great a Flame Aspires	541		248			
That Boy-Child of Mary	241					
The God of Abraham Praise	116	28				
Psalm 89:20-37						
Great Is Thy Faithfulness	140	30	81			
How Firm a Foundation	529	256				
I Will Call upon the Lord				2002		
Jesus Shall Reign Where'er the Sun	157					
Jesus, Name above All Names				2071		
My Gratitude Now Accept, O Lord				2044		
On Eagle's Wings	143		83			

Scripture Hymn Title	UMH	MVPC	CLUW	TFWS	SOZ	URW
Praise the Name of Jesus				2066		
The Care the Eagle Gives Her Young	118		302			199
We Sing to You, O God				2001		293

Ephesians 2:11-22

Scripture Hymn Title	UMH	MVPC	CLUW	TFWS	SOZ	URW
As We Gather at Your Table				2268		
Bind Us Together				2226		
Christ Is Made the Sure Foundation	559					
Christ Is the World's Light	188					
Christ, from Whom All Blessings Flow	550		250			
Come and Find the Quiet Center				2128		
Come Now, O Prince of Peace (O-so-so)			148	2232		415
For One Great Peace				2185		
Hail, Thou Once Despised Jesus	325					
He Came Down				2085		
He Is Exalted				2070		
Hope of the World	178					
How Firm a Foundation	529	256				
How Like a Gentle Spirit	115		216			
I Love Thy Kingdom, Lord	540					
In Christ There Is No East or West	548				65	
It Is Well with My Soul (When Peace, Like a River, Attendeth My Way)	377	250	304		20	
Just a Closer Walk with Thee				2158	46	
Just as I Am, Without One Plea	357				208	
Lord, Whose Love Through Humble Service	581					204
Now It Is Evening				2187		
O Church of God, United	547		249			
People Need the Lord				2244		
Sacred the Body				2228		
Sacred the Body				2228		
Sanctuary				2164		
See How Great a Flame Aspires	541		248			
The Church's One Foundation	545	269	255			
The Church's One Foundation	546					
Together We Serve				2175		
We Are God's People				2220		
We Are the Body of Christ				2227		

Scripture Hymn Title	UMH	MVPC	CLUW	TFWS	SOZ	URW
When Cain Killed Abel				2135		
You Are Mine				2218		

Mark 6:30-34, 53-56

Scripture Hymn Title	UMH	MVPC	CLUW	TFWS	SOZ	URW
Break Thou the Bread of Life	599					
Come and Find the Quiet Center				2128		
Come Away with Me				2202		59
Come, My Way, My Truth, My Life	164					
Dear Lord and Father of Mankind	358					
Fill My Cup, Lord	641					
Heal Us, Emmanuel, Hear Our Prayer	266		328			
Hope of the World	178					
Kum Ba Yah, My Lord	494		332		139	
Near to the Heart of God (There Is a Place of Quiet Rest)	472		324			
People Need the Lord				2244		
Prayer Is the Soul's Sincere Desire	492					
Rise, Shine, You People	187					
Savior, Like a Shepherd Lead Us	381					
Tell Me the Stories of Jesus	277		177			
The King of Love My Shepherd Is	138					
The Lord's My Shepherd, I'll Not Want	136		115			
Where Cross the Crowded Ways of Life	427	296				

July 26, 2009 (Eighth Sunday after Pentecost)

Liturgical Color: Green

Scripture Hymn Title	UMH	MVPC	CLUW	TFWS	SOZ	URW
2 Samuel 11:1-15						
Come Back Quickly to the Lord	343		272			
Forgive Us, Lord				2134		
Give Me a Clean Heart				2133	182	
I Need Thee Every Hour	397					
I Want a Principle Within	410					
It's Me, It's Me, O Lord	352		326		110	
O Jesus, I Have Promised	396	214				
We Utter Our Cry	439					
What Does the Lord Require	441					
Your Love, O God	120	26				
Psalm 14						
Abide with Me; Fast Falls the Eventide	700					
Amazing Grace! How Sweet the Sound	378	203	94		211	
Bless the Lord				2013		377
Creator of the Earth and Skies	450					
God Weeps				2048		
Holy Spirit, Come to Us				2118		395
Honor and Praise				2018		
Humble Thyself in the Sight of the Lord				2131		
If It Had Not Been for the Lord				2053		
Jesus, Savior, Lord (Saranam, Saranam)	523		105			
My Lord, What a Morning	719		386		145	
Now Praise the Hidden God of Love				2027		
O Day of God, Draw Nigh	730					
One God and Father of Us All				2240		
Praise the Source of Faith and Learning				2004		

143

Scripture Hymn Title	UMH	MVPC	CLUW	TFWS	SOZ	URW
Righteous and Just Is the Word of Our Lord (La Palabra Del Señor Es Recta)	107					
Seek the Lord Who Now Is Present	124					
Steal Away to Jesus	704		378		134	
We Believe in One True God	85					

Ephesians 3:14-21

Awake, O Sleeper, Rise from Death	551					
Bring Many Names				2047		
Celebrate Love				2073		
Christ Beside Me				2166		
Come Down, O Love Divine	475					
Creating God, Your Fingers Trace	109					
How Can We Name a Love	111					
How Can We Sinners Know	372		288			
Jesus Loves Me! This I Know	191	314	342		17	
Jesus, the Very Thought of Thee	175					
Jesus, Thine All-Victorious Love	422					
Just as I Am, Without One Plea	357				208	
Lord, Be Glorified				2150		
Love Divine, All Loves Excelling	384					100
Now Praise the Hidden God of Love				2027		
O Breath of Life, Come Sweeping through Us	543					
O Come and Dwell in Me	388					
O Lord, Your Tenderness				2143		
O Love, How Deep, How Broad, How High	267					
O Perfect Love, All Human Thought Transcending	645					
O Spirit of the Living God	539					
O the Depth of Love Divine	627					
Our Parent, by Whose Name	447					
Spirit Song	347	190	91			
Thou Hidden Love of God	414					
When We Are Living (Pues Si Vivimos)	356	337	310			175
Where the Spirit of the Lord Is				2119		
Your Love, O God	120	26				

Scripture Hymn Title	UMH	MVPC	CLUW	TFWS	SOZ	URW

John 6:1-21

Scripture Hymn Title	UMH	MVPC	CLUW	TFWS	SOZ	URW
Amen, Amen				2072		
Break Thou the Bread of Life	599					
Come Away with Me				2202		59
Come, All of You	350					
Come, Let Us Eat	625					
Come, My Way, My Truth, My Life	164					
Eat This Bread, Drink This Cup	628					379
Eternal Father, Strong to Save				2191		
Fill My Cup, Lord	641					
Give to the Winds Thy Fears	129		282			
How Firm a Foundation	529	256				
Jesus, Lover of My Soul	479					
Jesus, Savior, Pilot Me	509				49	
Jesus, the Very Thought of Thee	175					
Lord, I Lift Your Name on High				2088		
O Food to Pilgrims Given	631					
O Sing a Song of Bethlehem	179					
Praise the Name of Jesus				2066		
Stand By Me	512					41
Take Our Bread	640		238			
Tell Me the Stories of Jesus	277		177			
The Storm Is Passing Over						58
Through It All	507		279			
When the Storms of Life Are Raging	512					
You Are Mine				2218		
You Satisfy the Hungry Heart	629					

August 2, 2009 (Ninth Sunday after Pentecost)

Liturgical Color: Green

Scripture Hymn Title	UMH	MVPC	CLUW	TFWS	SOZ	URW
2 Samuel 11:26–12:13a						
And Can It Be that I Should Gain	363	206	280			
Change My Heart, O God			278	2152		
Depth of Mercy! Can There Be	355		273			
Give Me a Clean Heart				2133	182	
I Want a Principle Within	410					
Just as I Am, Without One Plea	357				208	
Make Me a Captive, Lord	421					
O For a Heart to Praise My God	417					
We Utter Our Cry	439					
What Does the Lord Require	441					
What Does the Lord Require of You				2174		
Psalm 51:1-12						
Breathe on Me, Breath of God	420					167
Change My Heart, O God			278	2152		
Depth of Mercy! Can There Be	355		273			
Fix Me, Jesus	655				122	
Forgive Us, Lord				2134		
Give Me a Clean Heart				2133	182	
Have Thine Own Way, Lord!	382	213	327			
I Want a Principle Within	410					
Jesus, Lover of My Soul	479					
Jubilate, Servite				2017		383
Just as I Am, Without One Plea	357				208	
Let Us Pray to the Lord	485					
O For a Heart to Praise My God	417					
Open Our Eyes				2086		

Scripture Hymn Title	UMH	MVPC	CLUW	TFWS	SOZ	URW
Pass Me Not, O Gentle Savior	351		271			
Please Enter My Heart, Hosanna				2154		
Sunday's Palms Are Wednesday's Ashes				2138		
Thy Holy Wings, O Savior	502					

Ephesians 4:1-16

Scripture Hymn Title	UMH	MVPC	CLUW	TFWS	SOZ	URW
All Praise to Our Redeeming Lord	554					
Awake, O Sleeper, Rise from Death	551					
Blest Be the Tie that Binds	557	347				
Forgive Our Sins as We Forgive	390					
Forward Through the Ages	555					
Help Us Accept Each Other	560		253			
I Sing a Song of the Saints of God	712					
In Unity We Lift Our Song				2221		
Let All Mortal Flesh Keep Silence	626		150		217	
Life-giving Bread				2261		
Lord, I Lift Your Name on High				2088		
Lord, You Give the Great Commission	584					
Make Us One				2224		
Many Gifts, One Spirit	114		212			
O Church of God, United	547		249			
One Bread, One Body	620	324	237			
One God and Father of Us All				2240		
Onward, Christian Soldiers	575	275				
The Church's One Foundation	545	269	255			
The Summons				2130		60
They'll Know We Are Christians by Our Love (We Are One in the Spirit)			257	2223		
Together We Serve				2175		
We Are God's People				2220		
We Are One in Christ Jesus				2229		
We Are the Body of Christ				2227		
When Our Confidence Is Shaken	505					

John 6:24-35

Scripture Hymn Title	UMH	MVPC	CLUW	TFWS	SOZ	URW
As We Gather at Your Table				2268		
Become to Us the Living Bread	630					
Blessed Jesus, at Thy Word	596		108			

Scripture Hymn Title	UMH	MVPC	CLUW	TFWS	SOZ	URW
Bread of the World in Mercy Broken	624		240			
Break Thou the Bread of Life	599					
Come, All of You	350					
Come, Let Us Eat	625					
Come, Sinners, to the Gospel Feast *Communion*	616					
Come, Sinners, to the Gospel Feast *Invitation*	339		88			
Deck Thyself, My Soul, with Gladness	612					
Eat This Bread and Never Hunger						122
Eat This Bread, Drink This Cup	628					379
Fill My Cup, Lord	641					
Forth in Thy Name, O Lord, I Go	438					
Gather Us In				2236		54
God Be with You till We Meet Again (GOD BE WITH YOU)	672	347		37		
God Be with You till We Meet Again (RANDOLPH)	673					
Guide Me, O Thou Great Jehovah	127					
Hallelujah! We Sing Your Praises						400
Here, O My Lord, I See Thee	623					
In the Singing				2255		
In Unity We Lift Our Song				2221		
Jesus, Joy of Our Desiring	644		344			
Jesus, Name above All Names				2071		
Lamb of God (Agnus Dei #2)						414
Let Us Be Bread				2260		
Let Us Break Bread Together	618	316	236		88	
Life-giving Bread				2261		
Light of the World				2204		
Mothering God, You Gave Me Birth				2050		
O Food to Pilgrims Given	631					
The Lily of the Valley				2062		
When the Poor Ones (Cuando El Pobre)	434	301	138			
You Satisfy the Hungry Heart	629					
You Who Are Thirsty				2132		

August 9, 2009 (Tenth Sunday after Pentecost)

Liturgical Color: Green

Scripture Hymn Title	UMH	MVPC	CLUW	TFWS	SOZ	URW
2 Samuel 18:5-9, 15, 31-33						
Abide with Me; Fast Falls the Eventide	700					
Be Still, My Soul	534	307				
Come, Ye Disconsolate, Where'er Ye Languish	510					
Dear Lord, for All in Pain	458					
God Be with You till We Meet Again (GOD BE WITH YOU)	672	347		37		
God Be with You till We Meet Again (RANDOLPH)	673					
God, How Can We Forgive				2169		
If Thou But Suffer God to Guide Thee	142					
Kyrie				2275		
O God Who Shaped Creation	443					
Out of the Depths				2136		
Out of the Depths I Cry to You	515					
Precious Lord, Take My Hand	474	309		179		
The Lord's My Shepherd, I'll Not Want	136	115				
Why Has God Forsaken Me?				2110		
Psalm 130						
Abide with Me; Fast Falls the Eventide	700					
Be Still, My Soul	534	307				
Canticle of Redemption	516					
Cares Chorus				2215		
Come and Find the Quiet Center				2128		
Dear Lord, for All in Pain	458					
Not So in Haste, My Heart	455					
O Lord, Hear My Prayer				2200		390

Scripture Hymn Title	UMH	MVPC	CLUW	TFWS	SOZ	URW
Out of the Depths				2136		
Out of the Depths I Cry to You	515					
Out of the Direst Depths (Psalm 130)						328
People Need the Lord				2244		
Precious Lord, Take My Hand	474	309			179	
Why Has God Forsaken Me?				2110		

Ephesians 4:25–5:2

Scripture Hymn Title	UMH	MVPC	CLUW	TFWS	SOZ	URW
All Praise to Thee, My God, This Night	682					213
As We Gather at Your Table				2268		
Baptized in Water				2248		
Forgive Our Sins as We Forgive	390					
God Made from One Blood				2170		
Healer of Our Every Ill				2213		161
Help Us Accept Each Other	560	253				
Holy, Holy				2039		
Hope of the World	178					
I Love Thy Kingdom, Lord	540					
I've Got Peace Like a River				2145		
Let There Be Peace on Earth	431	137				
Love Divine, All Loves Excelling	384					100
Loving Spirit				2123		203
Make Me a Channel of Your Peace				2171		
More Like You				2167		
O How He Loves You and Me				2108		
O Master, Let Me Walk with Thee	430	315				
Take My Life, and Let It Be Consecrated	399	312				
The Fragrance of Christ				2205		
This Is the Spirit's Entry Now	608					
Where Charity and Love Prevail	549					
Woke Up This Morning				2082		

John 6:35, 41-51

Scripture Hymn Title	UMH	MVPC	CLUW	TFWS	SOZ	URW
All Who Hunger				2126		
Become to Us the Living Bread	630					
Bread of the World in Mercy Broken	624	240				
Come, Sinners, to the Gospel Feast *Communion*	616					

Scripture Hymn Title	UMH	MVPC	CLUW	TFWS	SOZ	URW
Come, Ye Disconsolate, Where'er Ye Languish	510					
Deck Thyself, My Soul, with Gladness	612					
Eat This Bread and Never Hunger						122
Eat This Bread, Drink This Cup	628					379
Fill My Cup, Lord	641					
Gather Us In				2236		54
God the Sculptor of the Mountains				2060		
Hallelujah! We Sing Your Praises						400
Happy the One						212
Here, O My Lord, I See Thee	623					
Hope of the World	178					
I Received the Living God						137
Jesus, Joy of Our Desiring	644		344			
Jesus, Name above All Names				2071		
Lamb of God (Agnus Dei #2)						414
Let Us Break Bread Together	618	316	236		88	
Light of the World				2204		
Mothering God, You Gave Me Birth				2050		
O Food to Pilgrims Given	631					
The Bread of Life for All Is Broken	633					
The Lily of the Valley				2062		
Time Now to Gather				2265		
What Feast of Love						119
You Satisfy the Hungry Heart	629					
You Who Are Thirsty				2132		

August 16, 2009 (Eleventh Sunday after Pentecost)

Liturgical Color: Green

Scripture Hymn Title	UMH	MVPC	CLUW	TFWS	SOZ	URW
1 Kings 2:10-12; 3:3-14						
A Charge to Keep I Have	413					
Be Thou My Vision	451	240				180
Canticle of Wisdom	112					
Great Is Thy Faithfulness	140	30	81			
Lead Me, Lord	473					226
Lord, Speak to Me, that I May Speak	463					
Make Me a Servant				2176		
O Holy Spirit, Root of Life				2121		79
O Master, Let Me Walk with Thee	430		315			
O Word of God Incarnate	598					
Open My Eyes, that I May See	454	184				
What Does the Lord Require	441					
Psalm 111						
All My Hope Is Firmly Grounded	132					
Amen, We Praise Your Name, O God (Amen Siakudumisa)				2067		398
Awesome God				2040		
Great Is the Lord				2022		
Great Is Thy Faithfulness	140	30	81			
I'll Praise My Maker While I've Breath	60		123			
In the Lord I'll Be Ever Thankful				2195		381
Nothing Can Trouble				2054		388
O Holy Spirit, Root of Life				2121		79
O Master, Let Me Walk with Thee	430		315			
O Worship the King, All-Glorious Above	73					
Praise the Lord Who Reigns Above	96		124			

Scripture	Hymn Title	UMH	MVPC	CLUW	TFWS	SOZ	URW
	Praise the Source of Faith and Learning				2004		
	Sing Praise to God Who Reigns Above	126		60			70
	Thank You, Lord	84				228	
	Thou Art Worthy				2041		
	We, Thy People, Praise Thee	67	72				
	What a Mighty God We Serve				2021		

Ephesians 5:15-20

Scripture	Hymn Title	UMH	MVPC	CLUW	TFWS	SOZ	URW
	All Who Love and Serve Your City	433					
	Filled with the Spirit's Power	537					
	Give Me the Faith Which Can Remove	650					
	Give Thanks			247	2036		
	I'll Praise My Maker While I've Breath	60	123				
	I'm Goin'a Sing When the Spirit Says Sing	333	223			81	
	In the Lord I'll Be Ever Thankful				2195		381
	In the Singing				2255		
	Let All Things Now Living				2008		
	O Holy Spirit, Root of Life				2121		79
	O Spirit of the Living God	539					
	O Worship the King, All-Glorious Above	73					
	Praise the Source of Faith and Learning				2004		
	Sacred the Body				2228		
	Spirit of God, Descend upon My Heart	500					
	Take Time to Be Holy	395					
	Thank You, Lord	84				228	
	We Are Singing\We Are Marching\ Siyahamba			2235			
	We Bring the Sacrifice of Praise				2031		
	What a Mighty God We Serve				2021		
	When in Our Music God Is Glorified	68	129				
	When We Are Called to Sing Your Praise				2216		

John 6:51-58

Scripture	Hymn Title	UMH	MVPC	CLUW	TFWS	SOZ	URW
	Become to Us the Living Bread	630					
	Bread of the World in Mercy Broken	624	240				
	Broken for Me				2263		
	Come, Let Us Eat	625					
	Come, My Way, My Truth, My Life	164					

Scripture Hymn Title	UMH	MVPC	CLUW	TFWS	SOZ	URW
Come, Sinners, to the Gospel Feast *Communion*	616					
Come, Sinners, to the Gospel Feast *Invitation*	339	88				
God the Sculptor of the Mountains				2060		
Here, O My Lord, I See Thee	623					
In Remembrance of Me				2254		
Light of the World				2204		
Now in This Banquet						121
O Food to Pilgrims Given	631					
Seed, Scattered and Sown						125
Taste and See				2267		258
The Hand of Heaven						124
The Lily of the Valley				2062		
You Satisfy the Hungry Heart	629					

August 23, 2009 (Twelfth Sunday after Pentecost)

Liturgical Color: Green

Scripture Hymn Title	UMH	MVPC	CLUW	TFWS	SOZ	URW
1 Kings 8:(1, 6, 10-11), 22-30, 41-43						
Do, Lord, Remember Me	527				119	
God Is Here	660					
Holy				2019		
Holy Ground				2272		
I Sing Praises to Your Name				2037		
Immortal, Invisible, God Only Wise	103	74				
Let All the World in Every Corner Sing	93					
Maker, in Whom We Live	88					
My Prayer Rises to Heaven	498					
O God in Heaven, Grant to Thy Children	119	227				
Praise the Lord Who Reigns Above	96	124				
Remember Me, Remember Me	491		234		235	
Surely the Presence of the Lord Is in This Place	328	344	215			
Psalm 84						
All I Need Is You				2080		
As the Deer			116	2025		267
Blessed Quietness				2142	206	
Come, We that Love the Lord (Marching to Zion)	733				3	13
Come, We that Love the Lord (St. Thomas)	732					
Cry of My Heart				2165		
How Lovely, Lord, How Lovely				2042		
I Love Thy Kingdom, Lord	540					
I've Just Come from the Fountain				2250		
Mothering God, You Gave Me Birth				2050		

Scripture Hymn Title	UMH	MVPC	CLUW	TFWS	SOZ	URW
My Prayer Rises to Heaven	498					
Sing Alleluia to the Lord				2258		404
Surely the Presence of the Lord Is in This Place	328	344	215			
Without Seeing You				2206		
You Are My Hiding Place				2055		

Ephesians 6:10-20

Scripture Hymn Title	UMH	MVPC	CLUW	TFWS	SOZ	URW
A Mighty Fortress Is Our God	110	25				271
Be Thou My Vision	451	240				180
Come Away with Me				2202		59
Go Forth for God	670					
Hope of the World	178					
Lead On, O King Eternal	580	174				
May You Run and Not Be Weary				2281		451
O God of Every Nation	435					
Onward, Christian Soldiers	575	275				
Sent Out in Jesus' Name				2184		
Soldiers of Christ, Arise	513					
Stand Up, Stand Up for Jesus	514					
Standing on the Promises of Christ My King	374	252				
The Fragrance of Christ				2205		
You Are My Hiding Place				2055		

John 6:56-69

Scripture Hymn Title	UMH	MVPC	CLUW	TFWS	SOZ	URW
Become to Us the Living Bread	630					
Blessed Assurance, Jesus Is Mine!	369	65	287			
Blessed Jesus, at Thy Word	596	108				
Break Thou the Bread of Life	599					
Broken for Me				2263		
Here Is Bread, Here Is Wine				2266		
Hope of the World	178					
I Know Whom I Have Believed (I Know Not Why God's Wondrous Grace)	714		290			
In Remembrance of Me				2254		
Life-giving Bread				2261		
My Life Is in You, Lord				2032		
O Food to Pilgrims Given	631					
O the Depth of Love Divine	627					

Scripture Hymn Title	UMH	MVPC	CLUW	TFWS	SOZ	URW
O Word of God Incarnate	598					
Rise Up, O Men of God	576					
Send Your Word	195		113			
Spirit of Faith, Come Down	332		219			
Time Now to Gather				2265		
'Tis So Sweet to Trust in Jesus	462					
We Believe in One True God	85					
Wonderful Words of Life (Oh! Cantadmelas otra vez)	600	313				
Word of God, Come Down on Earth	182					

August 30, 2009 (Thirteenth Sunday after Pentecost)

Liturgical Color: Green

Scripture Hymn Title	UMH	MVPC	CLUW	TFWS	SOZ	URW
Song of Solomon 2:8-13						
As Man and Woman We Were Made	642					
Come, My Way, My Truth, My Life	164					
I Love You, Lord				2068		
Jesus, Joy of Our Desiring	644		344			
Jesus, Name above All Names				2071		
Jesus, the Very Thought of Thee	175					
Spirit Song	347	190	91			
The Gift of Love (Though I May Speak with Bravest Fire)	408		341		141	
The Lily of the Valley				2062		
When Love Is Found	643		343			
Your Love, O God, Has Called Us Here	647					
Psalm 45:1-2, 6-9 or Psalm 72 (UMH 795)						
As Man and Woman We Were Made	642					
Fairest Lord Jesus, Ruler of All Nature	189	63				
Honor and Praise				2018		
I Love You, Lord				2068		
Jesus, Joy of Our Desiring	644		344			
Majesty, Worship His Majesty	176	171	204			
Now Thank We All Our God	102					
O Lord, You're Beautiful				2064		
O Morning Star, How Fair and Bright	247					
The Day Thou Gavest, Lord, Is Ended	690					
The Gift of Love (Though I May Speak with Bravest Fire)	408		341		141	
When Love Is Found	643		343			
Your Love, O God, Has Called Us Here	647					

Scripture Hymn Title	UMH	MVPC	CLUW	TFWS	SOZ	URW
James 1:17-27						
Abide with Me; Fast Falls the Eventide	700					
All My Hope Is Firmly Grounded	132					
And Are We Yet Alive	553					
As the Sun Doth Daily Rise	675					
Blest Be the Dear Uniting Love	566		254			
Blest Be the Tie that Binds	557	347				
Come, Ye Thankful People, Come	694		241			
Father, We Thank You (ALBRIGHT)	563					
Father, We Thank You (RENDEZ À DIEU)	565					
For the Beauty of the Earth	92	8				
Gather Us In				2236		54
Give Thanks			247	2036		
Great Is Thy Faithfulness	140	30	81			
I Sing the Almighty Power of God	152		65			
I Want a Principle Within	410					
I Was There to Hear Your Borning Cry				2051		
Immortal, Invisible, God Only Wise	103		74			
In the Lord I'll Be Ever Thankful				2195		381
Lord, Be Glorified				2150		
Lord, I Want to Be a Christian	402	215			76	
Lord, Whose Love Through Humble Service	581					204
Make Me a Servant				2176		
O Beautiful for Spacious Skies	696					
O Young and Fearless Prophet	444					
Sent Forth By God's Blessing	664	366				
Sing a New Song to the Lord				2045		
Take My Life, and Let It Be Consecrated	399	312				
Together We Serve				2175		
We Are God's People				2220		
We Sing to You, O God				2001		293
Where Charity and Love Prevail	549					
Mark 7:1-8, 14-15, 21-23						
Canticle of Covenant Faithfulness	125					
Give Thanks			247	2036		
I Want a Principle Within	410					
Jesus, Thine All-Victorious Love	422					

Scripture Hymn Title	UMH	MVPC	CLUW	TFWS	SOZ	URW
Lord of the Dance (I Danced in the Morning)	261	128	170			
Lord, I Want to Be a Christian	402	215			76	
Love the Lord Your God				2168		
O For a Heart to Praise My God	417					
O Young and Fearless Prophet	444					
Open My Eyes, that I May See	454	184				
Open Our Eyes				2086		
Seek the Lord Who Now Is Present	124					

September 6, 2009 (Fourteenth Sunday after Pentecost)

Liturgical Color: Green

Scripture Hymn Title	UMH	MVPC	CLUW	TFWS SOZ	URW
Proverbs 22:1-2, 8-9, 22-23					
Change My Heart, O God			278	2152	
Lead Me, Guide Me				2214	
Lord, Whose Love Through Humble Service	581				204
Praise to the Lord				2029	309
Song of Hope				2186	
The Church of Christ, in Every Age	589				
The Voice of God Is Calling	436		139		
There's a Spirit in the Air	192				
Thy Word Is a Lamp unto My Feet	601		109		
When the Church of Jesus Shuts Its Outer Door	592				
When the Poor Ones (Cuando El Pobre)	434	301	138		
Where Cross the Crowded Ways of Life	427	296			
Wonderful Words of Life (Oh! Cantadmelas otra vez)	600	313			
Psalm 125 or Psalm 124 (UMH 846)					
Cares Chorus				2215	
Change My Heart, O God			278	2152	
Children of the Heavenly Father	141		335		
Goodness Is Stronger than Evil				2219	436
I Will Trust in the Lord	464		292	14	
Sanctuary				2164	
Trust and Obey (When We Walk with the Lord)	467		320		
We, Thy People, Praise Thee	67		72		

Scripture Hymn Title	UMH	MVPC	CLUW	TFWS	SOZ	URW
James 2:1-10, (11-13), 14-17						
Change My Heart, O God			278	2152		
Forgive Our Sins as We Forgive	390					
Forth in Thy Name, O Lord, I Go	438					
Gather Us In				2236		54
Give Thanks			247	2036		
Go Forth for God	670					
Healer of Our Every Ill				2213		161
In Christ There Is No East or West	548				65	
Jesu, Jesu, Fill Us with Your Love	432	288	179			116
Living for Jesus				2149		
Lord, Whose Love Through Humble Service	581					204
Make Me a Servant				2176		
Now Let Us from This Table Rise	634					
O Crucified Redeemer	425					
Sent Forth By God's Blessing	664		366			
Song of Hope				2186		
Sunday's Palms Are Wednesday's Ashes				2138		
Taste and See				2267		258
The Church of Christ, in Every Age	589					
Together We Serve				2175		
When the Church of Jesus Shuts Its Outer Door	592					
When the Poor Ones (Cuando El Pobre)	434	301	138			
Where Cross the Crowded Ways of Life	427	296				
Within the Day-to-Day				2245		
Mark 7:24-37						
Awesome God				2040		
Cares Chorus				2215		
Come, Ye Disconsolate, Where'er Ye Languish	510					
Dear Lord, for All in Pain	458					
He Touched Me (Shackled by a Heavy Burden)	367	209	286		72	
Heal Me, Hands of Jesus	262					
Heal Us, Emmanuel, Hear Our Prayer	266		328			
Jesus' Hands Were Kind Hands	273		176			

Scripture	Hymn Title	UMH	MVPC	CLUW	TFWS	SOZ	URW
	Lord, Whose Love Through Humble Service	581					204
	Mil Voces Para Celebrar	59					
	O Christ, the Healer, We Have Come	265					
	O For a Thousand Tongues to Sing	57	1	226			
	O Lord, You're Beautiful				2064		
	Oh, I Know the Lord's Laid His Hands on Me				2139		
	Open Our Eyes				2086		
	Rise, Shine, You People	187					
	Song of Hope				2186		
	Together We Serve				2175		
	What a Friend We Have in Jesus	526	257	333			
	When Jesus the Healer Passed Through Galilee	263		171			
	When the Poor Ones (Cuando El Pobre)	434	301	138			
	Your Song of Love						149

September 13, 2009 (Fifteenth Sunday after Pentecost)

Liturgical Color: Green

Scripture Hymn Title	UMH	MVPC	CLUW	TFWS	SOZ	URW
Proverbs 1:20-33						
All My Hope Is Firmly Grounded	132					
Be Thou My Vision	451	240				180
Canticle of Covenant Faithfulness	125					
Canticle of Wisdom	112					
Forgive Us, Lord				2134		
If Thou But Suffer God to Guide Thee	142					
I'm Gonna Live So God Can Use Me				2153		
O Word of God Incarnate	598					
Open My Eyes, that I May See	454	184				
Seek the Lord Who Now Is Present	124					
Psalm 19						
Alleluia	186		355			
As the Deer			116	2025		267
Awesome God				2040		
Creating God, Your Fingers Trace						67
For the Music of Creation						64
From All that Dwell Below the Skies	101		126			
God Created Heaven and Earth	151					
God, Who Stretched the Spangled Heavens	150		64			84
Great Is the Lord				2022		
Holy, Holy, Holy! Lord God Almighty	64	4	79			
How Great Thou Art	77	2	61			
I Love You, Lord				2068		
I Will Call upon the Lord				2002		
Jesus Shall Reign Where'er the Sun	157					
Let All Things Now Living				2008		

Scripture Hymn Title	UMH	MVPC	CLUW	TFWS	SOZ	URW
Let Us with a Joyful Mind				2012		
Let's Sing Unto the Lord (Cantemos al Señor)	149	49	67			
More Precious than Silver				2065		
My Life Flows On				2212		170
Now, on Land and Sea Descending	685		372			
O Crucified Redeemer	425					
Praise the Name of Jesus				2066		
Praise the Source of Faith and Learning				2004		
Psalm 19:1-6						240
Psalm 19:7-14						241
This Is My Father's World	144	47	62			71
This Is the Day the Lord Hath Made (Twenty-Fourth)	658					
Thy Word Is a Lamp unto My Feet	601		109			
To Know You More				2161		
We Sing of Your Glory				2011		
Wonderful Words of Life (Oh! Cantadmelas otra vez)	600	313				

James 3:1-12

Scripture Hymn Title	UMH	MVPC	CLUW	TFWS	SOZ	URW
How Like a Gentle Spirit	115		216			
I Will Call upon the Lord				2002		
I'm Goin' a Sing When the Spirit Says Sing	333		223		81	
Lord, Speak to Me, that I May Speak	463					
Make Me a Channel of Your Peace				2171		
More Like You				2167		
Sing Praise to God Who Reigns Above	126		60			70
Take My Life, and Let It Be Consecrated	399		312			
Where Charity and Love Prevail	549					
Woke Up This Morning				2082		

Mark 8:27-38

Scripture Hymn Title	UMH	MVPC	CLUW	TFWS	SOZ	URW
All I Need Is You				2080		
And Are We Yet Alive	553					
Be Thou My Vision	451	240				180
Beneath the Cross of Jesus	297					
Christ for the World We Sing	568		260			

Scripture Hymn Title	UMH	MVPC	CLUW	TFWS	SOZ	URW
Come, Ye Thankful People, Come	694		241			
Cry of My Heart				2165		
Faith, While Trees Are Still in Blossom	508		97			
Father, I Adore You			225	2038		
Forth in Thy Name, O Lord, I Go	438					
Hail, Thou Once Despised Jesus	325					
He Is Lord, He Is Lord!	177	173				233
I Can Hear My Savior Calling	338					
I Have Decided to Follow Jesus				2129		
Jesus Calls Us o'er the Tumult	398		96			
Jesus, Draw Me Close				2159		
Lift High the Cross	159	164	174			
Living for Jesus				2149		
Lord of the Dance (I Danced in the Morning)	261	128	170			
Lord, Have Mercy				2277		
Morning Has Broken	145	354	370			186
Must Jesus Bear the Cross Alone	424					
My Song Is Love Unknown				2083		
Nearer, My God, to Thee	528		308			
Praise the Lord Who Reigns Above	96		124			
Rejoice, Ye Pure in Heart (MARION)	160		130			
Rejoice, Ye Pure in Heart (VINEYARD HAVEN)	161					
Swiftly Pass the Clouds of Glory				2102		
Take Up Thy Cross, the Savior Said	415		145			
That Boy-Child of Mary	241					
The Church of Christ, in Every Age	589					
The God of Abraham Praise	116	28				
The Summons				2130		60
Two Fishermen				2101		
Weary of All Trumpeting	442					
Where He Leads Me	338					42
Within the Day-to-Day				2245		
Would I Have Answered When You Called				2137		

September 20, 2009 (Sixteenth Sunday after Pentecost)

Liturgical Color: Green

Scripture Hymn Title	UMH	MVPC	CLUW	TFWS	SOZ	URW
Proverbs 31:10-31						
All Who Love and Serve Your City	433					
Dear Jesus, in Whose Life I See	468					
Forth in Thy Name, O Lord, I Go	438					
Happy the Home When God Is there	445					
I Sing a Song of the Saints of God	712					
I'm Gonna Live So God Can Use Me				2153		
Lord, Be Glorified				2150		
Morning Glory, Starlit Sky	194					
O Lord, May Church and Home Combine	695					
O Word of God Incarnate	598					
Our Parent, by Whose Name	447					
Sing of Mary, Pure and Lowly	272					
The First One Ever, Oh, Ever to Know	276					
Woman in the Night	274					
Psalm 1						
A Charge to Keep I Have	413					
All My Hope Is Firmly Grounded	132					
Blessed Jesus, at Thy Word	596	108				
Guide My Feet				2208		
Happy Are They (Psalm 1)						223
Happy Is the One (Psalm 1)						224
He Has Made Me Glad				2270		
If Thou But Suffer God to Guide Thee	142					
Lead Me, Guide Me				2214		
Love the Lord Your God				2168		
My Life Is in You, Lord				2032		

Scripture Hymn Title	UMH	MVPC	CLUW	TFWS	SOZ	URW
Nothing Can Trouble				2054		388
O Blessed Spring				2076		
O Word of God Incarnate	598					
On Eagle's Wings	143		83			
Praise the Name of Jesus				2066		
Praise the Source of Faith and Learning				2004		
Righteous and Just Is the Word of Our Lord (La Palabra Del Señor Es Recta)	107					
Seek the Lord Who Now Is Present	124					
The First Song of Isaiah				2030		
The Lone, Wild Bird				2052		
Through It All	507		279			
Thy Word Is a Lamp unto My Feet	601		109			

James 3:13–4:3, 7-8a

Scripture Hymn Title	UMH	MVPC	CLUW	TFWS	SOZ	URW
Blessed Assurance, Jesus Is Mine!	369	65	287			
Close to Thee	407					7
Come Down, O Love Divine	475					
For One Great Peace				2185		
Holy Spirit, Truth Divine	465					
How Like a Gentle Spirit	115		216			
Humble Thyself in the Sight of the Lord				2131		
I Am Thine, O Lord	419	218				
I Need Thee Every Hour	397					
I Surrender All	354	225			67	
Jesus, Draw Me Close				2159		
Jesus, Lord, We Look to Thee	562					
Jesus, United by Thy Grace	561					
Just a Closer Walk with Thee				2158	46	
Let There Be Peace on Earth	431		137			
Living for Jesus				2149		
Lord, I Want to Be a Christian	402	215			76	
Make Me a Channel of Your Peace				2171		
Near to the Heart of God (There Is a Place of Quiet Rest)	472		324			
O Come, O Come, Emmanuel	211	80				
O Crucified Redeemer	425					

Scripture Hymn Title	UMH	MVPC	CLUW	TFWS	SOZ	URW
O For a Heart to Praise My God	417					
O Word of God Incarnate	598					
Praise the Source of Faith and Learning				2004		
Source and Sovereign, Rock and Cloud	113					
They'll Know We Are Christians by Our Love (We Are One in the Spirit)			257	2223		
Thou My Everlasting Portion	407					
Together We Serve				2175		
We Are Called				2172		
We Need a Faith				2181		
We Utter Our Cry	439					

Mark 9:30-37

Scripture Hymn Title	UMH	MVPC	CLUW	TFWS	SOZ	URW
All Who Love and Serve Your City	433					
Are Ye Able, Said the Master	530	300				
Dear Jesus, in Whose Life I See	468					
I Come with Joy to Meet My Lord	617					120
I Sing a Song of the Saints of God	712					
Jesu, Jesu, Fill Us with Your Love	432	288	179			116
Jesus Loves Me! This I Know	191	314	342		17	
Jesus, Lord, We Look to Thee	562					
Jesus, United by Thy Grace	561					
Like a Child				2092		
Lord, I Want to Be a Christian	402	215			76	
Lord, Whose Love Through Humble Service	581					204
Make Me a Captive, Lord	421					
Make Me a Servant				2176		
O For a Heart to Praise My God	417					
O Master, Let Me Walk with Thee	430		315			
The Church of Christ, in Every Age	589					
The Servant Song (Brother, Sister, Let Me Serve You)				2222		117
Together We Serve				2175		
What Does the Lord Require	441					
Where Charity and Love Prevail	549					

September 27, 2009 (Seventeenth Sunday after Pentecost)

Liturgical Color: Green

Scripture Hymn Title	UMH	MVPC	CLUW	TFWS	SOZ	URW
Esther 7:1-6, 9-10; 9:20-22						
All People that on Earth Do Dwell	75		118			
Come, Ye Disconsolate, Where'er Ye Languish	510					
Faith Is Patience in the Night				2211		
God of Many Names	105					
God, How Can We Forgive				2169		
His Eye Is on the Sparrow				2146	33	
If It Had Not Been for the Lord				2053		
Jesus, Savior, Lord (Saranam, Saranam)	523		105			
Joy Comes with the Dawn				2210		
O God, Our Help in Ages Past	117					200
Praise to the Lord, the Almighty	139	29	68			63
Righteous and Just Is the Word of Our Lord (La Palabra Del Señor Es Recta)	107					
Sing Praise to God Who Reigns Above	126		60			70
They'll Know We Are Christians by Our Love (We Are One in the Spirit)			257	2223		
We Sing to You, O God				2001		293
We, Thy People, Praise Thee	67		72			
Wellspring of Wisdom	506					173
Psalm 124						
All My Hope Is Firmly Grounded	132					
Blessed Be the Name of the Lord				2034		
By Gracious Powers So Wonderfully Sheltered	517					
Change My Heart, O God			278	2152		

Scripture	Hymn Title	UMH	MVPC	CLUW	TFWS	SOZ	URW
	Children of the Heavenly Father	141		335			
	Deep in the Shadows of the Past				2246		
	Go Forth for God	670					
	Great Is Thy Faithfulness	140	30	81			
	His Eye Is on the Sparrow				2146	33	
	I'll Praise My Maker While I've Breath	60		123			
	If It Had Not Been for the Lord				2053		
	Jesus, Savior, Lord (Saranam, Saranam)	523		105			
	Lift Every Voice and Sing	519				32	
	On Eagle's Wings	143		83			
	Praise to the Lord				2029		309
	Stand By Me	512				41	
	The First Song of Isaiah				2030		
	When the Storms of Life Are Raging	512					

James 5:13-20

Scripture	Hymn Title	UMH	MVPC	CLUW	TFWS	SOZ	URW
	Come Away with Me				2202		59
	Come Back Quickly to the Lord	343		272			
	Dear Lord, for All in Pain	458					
	Deep in the Shadows of the Past				2246		
	God, How Can We Forgive				2169		
	Let Us Offer to the Father				2262		
	Lord, Listen to Your Children Praying				2193		
	Make Me a Servant				2176		
	Prayer Is the Soul's Sincere Desire	492					
	Rescue the Perishing	591					
	Sing Praise to God Who Reigns Above	126		60			70
	Sweet Hour of Prayer	496	248	330			
	The Fragrance of Christ				2205		
	The Lord's Prayer				2278		453
	They'll Know We Are Christians by Our Love (We Are One in the Spirit)			257	2223		
	We Sing to You, O God				2001		293
	When in Our Music God Is Glorified	68		129			

Mark 9:38-50

Scripture	Hymn Title	UMH	MVPC	CLUW	TFWS	SOZ	URW
	A Charge to Keep I Have	413					
	Blessed Jesus, at Thy Word	596		108			
	Dear Lord, Lead Me Day by Day	411		100			

Scripture Hymn Title	UMH	MVPC	CLUW	TFWS	SOZ	URW
Deep in the Shadows of the Past				2246		
God of Grace and God of Glory	577	287				
Heal Us, Emmanuel, Hear Our Prayer	266		328			
How Shall They Hear the Word of God	649					
I Want a Principle Within	410					
Lord, Listen to Your Children Praying				2193		
Make Me a Servant				2176		
O Christ, the Healer, We Have Come	265					
Rescue the Perishing	591					
Sois la Semilla (You Are the Seed)	583	291				
The Lord's Prayer				2278		453
There's a Spirit in the Air	192					
Trust and Obey (When We Walk with the Lord)	467		320			
When the Poor Ones (Cuando El Pobre)	434	301	138			
Where Cross the Crowded Ways of Life	427	296				
Where the Spirit of the Lord Is				2119		

October 4, 2009 (Eighteenth Sunday after Pentecost)

Liturgical Color: Green

Scripture Hymn Title	UMH	MVPC	CLUW	TFWS	SOZ	URW
Job 1:1; 2:1-10						
All My Hope Is Firmly Grounded	132					
Blessed Be the Name	63					
By Gracious Powers So Wonderfully Sheltered	517					
Faith Is Patience in the Night				2211		
Give to the Winds Thy Fears	129		282			
How Firm a Foundation	529	256				
I Want Jesus to Walk with Me	521		104		95	110
I Will Trust in the Lord	464		292		14	
Jesus, Tempted in the Desert				2105		
Lift Every Voice and Sing	519				32	
My Hope Is Built on Nothing Less	368	261				
My Life Is in You, Lord				2032		
My Tribute	99					
Nobody Knows the Trouble I See	520				170	
Precious Lord, Take My Hand	474		309		179	
Rejoice in God's Saints	708					
Through It All	507		279			
We'll Understand It Better By and By	525	317			55	
Wellspring of Wisdom	506					173
When Our Confidence Is Shaken	505					
Psalm 26 or Psalm 25 (UMH 756)						
Canticle of the Holy Trinity	80					
Children of the Heavenly Father	141		335			
Cry of My Heart				2165		
How Firm a Foundation	529	256				

Scripture Hymn Title	UMH	MVPC	CLUW	TFWS	SOZ	URW
I Love Thy Kingdom, Lord	540					
I Want Jesus to Walk with Me	521		104		95	110
I Will Trust in the Lord	464		292		14	
Lead Me, Lord	473					226
My Hope Is Built on Nothing Less	368	261				
My Prayer Rises to Heaven	498					
O Lord, Hear My Prayer				2200		390
Precious Lord, Take My Hand	474		309		179	

Hebrews 1:1-4; 2:5-12

Scripture Hymn Title	UMH	MVPC	CLUW	TFWS	SOZ	URW
All Hail the Power of Jesus' Name (Coronation)	154	60				
All Hail the Power of Jesus' Name (Diadem)	155					
All Praise to Thee, for Thou, O King Divine	166					
And Can It Be that I Should Gain	363	206	280			
At the Name of Jesus Every Knee Shall Bow	168					
Canticle of Christ's Obedience	167					
Children of the Heavenly Father	141		335			
Crown Him with Many Crowns	327	157				
God Hath Spoken by the Prophets	108	38				
His Name Is Wonderful	174	172	203			
Holy God, We Praise Thy Name	79		80			
How Majestic Is Your Name				2023		
Jesus! the Name High over All	193		199			
Majesty, Worship His Majesty	176	171	204			
My Song Is Love Unknown				2083		
My Tribute	99					
O Love, How Deep, How Broad, How High	267					
Rejoice, the Lord Is King (Darwall's 148th)	715					
Rejoice, the Lord Is King (Gopsal)	716					
Shout to the Lord				2074		
The Head that Once Was Crowned with Thorns	326					
Thou Art Worthy				2041		
Ye Servants of God, Your Master Proclaim	181					

Scripture Hymn Title	UMH	MVPC	CLUW	TFWS	SOZ	URW

Mark 10:2-16

Scripture Hymn Title	UMH	MVPC	CLUW	TFWS	SOZ	URW
As Man and Woman We Were Made	642					
Children of the Heavenly Father	141		335			
God Is Here	660					
Happy the Home When God Is there	445					
How Blest Are They Who Trust in Christ	654					
Jesus Loves Me! This I Know	191	314	342		17	
Jesus, Lover of My Soul	479					
Jesus' Hands Were Kind Hands	273		176			
Like a Child				2092		
Lord of All Hopefulness				2197		179
Lord, We Come to Ask Your Blessing				2230		
O Lord, May Church and Home Combine	695					
O Perfect Love, All Human Thought Transcending	645					
Our Parent, by Whose Name	447					
Praise the One Who Breaks the Darkness						90
Tell Me the Stories of Jesus	277		177			
When Love Is Found	643		343			
Where Children Belong				2233		
Within the Day-to-Day				2245		

October 11, 2009 (Nineteenth Sunday after Pentecost)

Liturgical Color: Green

Scripture Hymn Title	UMH	MVPC	CLUW	TFWS	SOZ	URW
Job 23:1-9, 16-17						
Come Down, O Love Divine	475					
Dear Lord, for All in Pain	458					
Do, Lord, Remember Me	527				119	
Goodness Is Stronger than Evil				2219		436
How Long, O Lord				2209		
Jesus, Tempted in the Desert				2105		
Kum Ba Yah, My Lord	494		332		139	
My Faith Looks Up to Thee	452				215	
Nobody Knows the Trouble I See	520				170	
Not So in Haste, My Heart	455					
Out of the Depths I Cry to You	515					
Precious Lord, Take My Hand	474		309		179	
Rejoice in God's Saints	708					
Why Stand So Far Away, My God?				2180		
Psalm 22:1-15						
Come Down, O Love Divine	475					
Give Thanks			247	2036		
God Will Take Care of You (Nunca desmayes)	130	260				
How Long, O Lord				2209		
I Want Jesus to Walk with Me	521		104		95	110
I Will Trust in the Lord	464		292		14	
Jesus, Tempted in the Desert				2105		
Lead Me, Lord	473					226
Let Us Plead for Faith Alone	385					
My Faith Looks Up to Thee	452				215	
Nobody Knows the Trouble I See	520				170	

Scripture	Hymn Title	UMH	MVPC	CLUW	TFWS	SOZ	URW
	O Sacred Head, Now Wounded	286	139				
	Out of the Depths				2136		
	Out of the Depths I Cry to You	515					
	Praise, My Soul, the King of Heaven	66					75
	Precious Lord, Take My Hand	474		309		179	
	Remember Me, Remember Me	491		234		235	
	The God of Abraham Praise	116	28				
	Trust and Obey (When We Walk with the Lord)	467		320			
	Why Has God Forsaken Me?				2110		
	Why Stand So Far Away, My God?				2180		

Hebrews 4:12-16

Scripture	Hymn Title	UMH	MVPC	CLUW	TFWS	SOZ	URW
	Blessed Jesus, at Thy Word	596		108			
	By Gracious Powers So Wonderfully Sheltered	517					
	Canticle of Christ's Obedience	167					
	Come, Let Us with Our Lord Arise				2084		
	Come, Thou Almighty King	61	11				
	Come, Thou Fount of Every Blessing	400	42	127			92
	Come, Ye Disconsolate, Where'er Ye Languish	510					
	Crown Him with Many Crowns	327	157				
	Dear Jesus, in Whose Life I See	468					
	God, How Can We Forgive				2169		
	Grace Greater than Our Sin	365					
	He Came Down				2085		
	Hope of the World	178					
	Jesus, Lover of My Soul	479					
	Lead Me, Lord	473					226
	Lord, Have Mercy				2277		
	Marvelous Grace of Our Loving Lord	365					
	Mothering God, You Gave Me Birth				2050		
	O the Lamb, the Loving Lamb	300					
	O Word of God Incarnate	598					
	People Need the Lord				2244		
	Praise the One Who Breaks the Darkness						90
	There's a Wideness in God's Mercy	121					

Scripture Hymn Title	UMH	MVPC	CLUW	TFWS	SOZ	URW
Thy Word Is a Lamp unto My Feet	601		109			
What a Friend We Have in Jesus	526	257	333			
Womb of Life				2046		

Mark 10:17-31

Scripture Hymn Title	UMH	MVPC	CLUW	TFWS	SOZ	URW
A Mighty Fortress Is Our God	110	25				271
Come and See				2127		
Cry of My Heart				2165		
Dear Jesus, in Whose Life I See	468					
Deck Thyself, My Soul, with Gladness	612					
Give Thanks			247	2036		
Humble Thyself in the Sight of the Lord				2131		
I Have Decided to Follow Jesus				2129		
Jesus Calls Us o'er the Tumult	398		96			
Lord, I Want to Be a Christian	402	215			76	
Lord, Speak to Me, that I May Speak	463					
O God Who Shaped Creation	443					
O Jesus, I Have Promised	396	214				
O Master, Let Me Walk with Thee	430	315				
O Young and Fearless Prophet	444					
Rise Up, O Men of God	576					
Take My Life, and Let It Be Consecrated	399	312				
Take Up Thy Cross, the Savior Said	415	145				
The Summons				2130		60
Trust and Obey (When We Walk with the Lord)	467	320				
When We All Get to Heaven (Sing the Wondrous Love of Jesus)	701	383	381		15	
Would I Have Answered When You Called				2137		
You Are Mine				2218		

October 12, 2009 (Thanksgiving Day—Canada)

Liturgical Color: Red or White

Scripture Hymn Title	UMH	MVPC	CLUW	TFWS	SOZ	URW
Joel 2:21-27						
All Creatures of Our God and King	62	22				
Come, All of You	350					
Come, Ye Thankful People, Come	694		241			
Depth of Mercy! Can There Be	355		273			
Now Thank We All Our God	102					
Open Our Eyes				2086		
There's a Wideness in God's Mercy	121					
Una Espiga	637	319				
We Gather Together to Ask the Lord's Blessing	131	361				
We, Thy People, Praise Thee	67		72			
Psalm 126						
Bless His Holy Name				2015		
Come, Ye Disconsolate, Where'er Ye Languish	510					
Give to the Winds Thy Fears	129		282			
God Has Done Great Things for Us (Psalm 126)						326
Hail to the Lord's Anointed	203	81				
Joy Comes with the Dawn				2210		
Let's Sing Unto the Lord (Cantemos al Señor)	149	49	67			
O God, Our Help in Ages Past	117					200
O Spirit of the Living God	539					
Rejoice, Ye Pure in Heart (MARION)	160		130			
Rejoice, Ye Pure in Heart (VINEYARD HAVEN)	161					
The Trees of the Field				2279		

Scripture Hymn Title	UMH	MVPC	CLUW	TFWS	SOZ	URW
When God First Brought Us Back from Exile (Psalm 126)						325
When God Restored Our Common Life				2182		

1 Timothy 2:1-7

Scripture Hymn Title	UMH	MVPC	CLUW	TFWS	SOZ	URW
Christ Is the World's Light	188					
Come and Find the Quiet Center				2128		
Dona Nobis Pacem	376	360	142			443
Give Thanks			247	2036		
God of Many Names	105					
Jesus, Name above All Names				2071		
Let There Be Light	440					
Make Me a Channel of Your Peace				2171		
This Is My Song	437					
We Believe in One True God	85					

Matthew 6:25-33

Scripture Hymn Title	UMH	MVPC	CLUW	TFWS	SOZ	URW
All My Hope Is Firmly Grounded	132					
All Things Bright and Beautiful	147		63			
Be Still, My Soul	534		307			
Bring Forth the Kingdom				2190		
Cares Chorus				2215		
Children of the Heavenly Father	141		335			
For the Fruits of This Creation	97					193
Give Thanks			247	2036		
Give to the Winds Thy Fears	129		282			
God Be with You till We Meet Again (GOD BE WITH YOU)	672		347		37	
God Be with You till We Meet Again (RANDOLPH)	673					
God Is So Good				2056	231	
God Will Take Care of You (Nunca desmayes)	130	260				
Great Is Thy Faithfulness	140	30	81			
His Eye Is on the Sparrow				2146	33	
How Lovely, Lord, How Lovely				2042		
I Will Trust in the Lord	464		292		14	
If the World from You Withhold	522					

Scripture Hymn Title	UMH	MVPC	CLUW	TFWS	SOZ	URW
If Thou But Suffer God to Guide Thee	142					
Leave It There	522				23	
Praise Our God Above				2061		
Rise to Greet the Sun	678		371			
Seek Ye First the Kingdom of God	405	201	136			
Someone Asked the Question				2144		
You Satisfy the Hungry Heart	629					

October 18, 2009 (Twentieth Sunday after Pentecost)

Liturgical Color: Green

Scripture Hymn Title	UMH	MVPC	CLUW	TFWS	SOZ	URW
Job 38:1-7, (34-41)						
All Things Bright and Beautiful	147		63			
Eternal Father, Strong to Save				2191		
God of the Sparrow God of the Whale	122	37	59			
God, Who Stretched the Spangled Heavens	150		64			84
Great Is the Lord				2022		
How Great Thou Art	77	2	61			
I Sing the Almighty Power of God	152		65			
Immortal, Invisible, God Only Wise	103		74			
Joy Comes with the Dawn				2210		
Joyful, Joyful, We Adore Thee	89	5	75			65
Let All Things Now Living				2008		
Lord of the Dance (I Danced in the Morning)	261	128	170			
Many and Great, O God, Are Thy Things	148	50	71			232
O God Who Shaped Creation	443					
O Little Town of Bethlehem	230	94				
O Worship the King, All-Glorious Above	73					
Praise the Source of Faith and Learning				2004		
This Is My Father's World	144	47	62			71
Psalm 104:1-9, 24, 35c						
Bless the Lord				2013		377
Great Is the Lord				2022		
Immortal, Invisible, God Only Wise	103		74			
Joyful, Joyful, We Adore Thee	89	5	75			65
Let Us with a Joyful Mind				2012		
Maker, in Whom We Live	88					

Scripture Hymn Title	UMH	MVPC	CLUW	TFWS	SOZ	URW
Many and Great, O God, Are Thy Things	148	50	71			232
O Worship the King, All-Glorious Above	73					

Hebrews 5:1-10

Scripture Hymn Title	UMH	MVPC	CLUW	TFWS	SOZ	URW
Ah, Holy Jesus, How Hast Thou Offended	289		186			
Alas! and Did My Savior Bleed (HUDSON)	359	202			8	
Alas! and Did My Savior Bleed (MARTYRDOM)	294					
All Hail the Power of Jesus' Name (CORONATION)	154	60				
All Hail the Power of Jesus' Name (DIADEM)	155					
All Praise to Thee, for Thou, O King Divine	166					
At the Name of Jesus Every Knee Shall Bow	168					
Blessed Assurance, Jesus Is Mine!	369	65	287			
Blow Ye the Trumpet, Blow	379	309				
Crown Him with Many Crowns	327	157				
Glorious Things of Thee Are Spoken	731		256			
Hail, Thou Once Despised Jesus	325					
Hallelujah! What a Savior	165					
Humble Thyself in the Sight of the Lord				2131		
In Thee Is Gladness	169					
Jesus! the Name High over All	193		199			
Lift High the Cross	159	164	174			
Lord, I Lift Your Name on High				2088		
Love the Lord Your God				2168		
Make Me a Captive, Lord	421					
Man of Sorrows! What a Name	165					
My Song Is Love Unknown				2083		
Nothing But the Blood	362					
Now Praise the Hidden God of Love				2027		
O Love Divine, What Hast Thou Done	287		185			
O the Lamb, the Loving Lamb	300					
Rise, Shine, You People	187					
Rock of Ages, Cleft for Me	361	247				
Thou Didst Leave Thy Throne				172	2100	
'Tis Finished! The Messiah Dies	282		182			
Victim Divine				2259		

Scripture Hymn Title	UMH	MVPC	CLUW	TFWS	SOZ	URW
We Bring the Sacrifice of Praise				2031		
What Can Wash Away My Sin	362					

Mark 10:35-45

Scripture Hymn Title	UMH	MVPC	CLUW	TFWS	SOZ	URW
All Praise to Thee, for Thou, O King Divine	166					
Are Ye Able, Said the Master	530	300				
By Gracious Powers So Wonderfully Sheltered	517					
Christ, Be Our Light						114
Jesu, Jesu, Fill Us with Your Love	432	288	179			116
Life-giving Bread				2261		
Lord God, Your Love Has Called Us Here	579					
Lord, Whose Love Through Humble Service	581					204
Make Me a Captive, Lord	421					
Make Me a Channel of Your Peace				2171		
Make Me a Servant				2176		
Must Jesus Bear the Cross Alone	424					
Now Let Us from This Table Rise	634					
Now Praise the Hidden God of Love				2027		
O Master, Let Me Walk with Thee	430		315			
Take Up Thy Cross, the Savior Said	415		145			
The Servant Song (Brother, Sister, Let Me Serve You)				2222		117
The Summons				2130		60
There Is a Balm in Gilead	375	262	98		123	
Thou Didst Leave Thy Throne			172	2100		
Together We Serve				2175		
Two Fishermen				2101		
We Are the Church	558		252			
Ye Servants of God, Your Master Proclaim	181					

October 25, 2009 (Twenty-first Sunday after Pentecost)

Liturgical Color: Green

Scripture Hymn Title	UMH	MVPC	CLUW	TFWS	SOZ	URW
Job 42:1-6, 10-17						
All People that on Earth Do Dwell	75		118			
From All that Dwell Below the Skies	101		126			
Goodness Is Stronger than Evil				2219		436
Healer of Our Every Ill				2213		161
If Thou But Suffer God to Guide Thee	142					
Joyful, Joyful, We Adore Thee	89	5	75			65
O God Beyond All Praising				2009		
O God, Our Help in Ages Past	117					200
O Worship the King, All-Glorious Above	73					
People Need the Lord				2244		
Praise the Source of Faith and Learning				2004		
Praise, My Soul, the King of Heaven	66					75
Stand Up and Bless the Lord	662		128			
When Our Confidence Is Shaken	505					
Wonderful Words of Life (Oh! Cantadmelas otra vez)	600	313				
Wounded World that Cries for Healing				2177		
Psalm 34:1-8, (19-22)						
All Who Hunger				2126		
Bless His Holy Name				2015		
Blessed Be the God of Israel	209					12
Canticle of Love	646					
Come, Christians, Join to Sing	158					
Come, Let Us Use the Grace Divine	606					135
Come, Sinners, to the Gospel Feast Communion	616					

Scripture Hymn Title	UMH	MVPC	CLUW	TFWS	SOZ	URW
Come, Sinners, to the Gospel Feast *Invitation*	339		88			
How Majestic Is Your Name				2023		
If Thou But Suffer God to Guide Thee	142					
Jesus, Savior, Lord (Saranam, Saranam)	523		105			
Joyful, Joyful, We Adore Thee	89	5	75			65
Life-giving Bread				2261		
Lord, I Lift Your Name on High				2088		
O God Beyond All Praising				2009		
Praise the Name of Jesus				2066		
Shout to the Lord				2074		
Swing Low, Sweet Chariot	703		384		104	
Taste and See				2267		258
Tell Out, My Soul, the Greatness of the Lord!	200					
We, Thy People, Praise Thee	67		72			
What Feast of Love						119
You Who Are Thirsty				2132		

Hebrews 7:23-28

Ask Ye What Great Thing I Know	163					
Blow Ye the Trumpet, Blow	379	309				
Christ, Whose Glory Fills the Skies	173		281			
Come, Let Us Use the Grace Divine	606					135
Hail, Thou Once Despised Jesus	325					
In Thee Is Gladness	169					
Jesus, Name above All Names				2071		
My Hope Is Built on Nothing Less	368	261				
Nothing But the Blood	362					
O How I Love Jesus (There Is a Name I Love to Hear)	170		198		36	
O Lord, Hear My Prayer				2200		390
Praise, My Soul, the King of Heaven	66					75
Victory in Jesus	370		92			
We Walk by Faith				2196		
What Can Wash Away My Sin	362					
Wonderful Words of Life (Oh! Cantadmelas otra vez)	600	313				

Scripture Hymn Title	UMH	MVPC	CLUW	TFWS	SOZ	URW

Mark 10:46-52

Scripture Hymn Title	UMH	MVPC	CLUW	TFWS	SOZ	URW
An Outcast Among Outcasts				2104		
Be Thou My Vision	451	240				180
Depth of Mercy! Can There Be	355		273			
Give Me the Faith Which Can Remove	650					
Heal Me, Hands of Jesus	262					
Heal Us, Emmanuel, Hear Our Prayer	266		328			
Healer of Our Every Ill				2213		161
If Thou But Suffer God to Guide Thee	142					
Jesus' Hands Were Kind Hands	273		176			
Kyrie				2275		
Let Us Plead for Faith Alone	385					
Lord, Have Mercy				2277		
Mil Voces Para Celebrar	59					
My Faith Looks Up to Thee	452					215
O Christ, the Healer, We Have Come	265					
O For a Thousand Tongues to Sing	57	1	226			
O How I Love Jesus (There Is a Name I Love to Hear)	170		198		36	
Open My Eyes, that I May See	454	184				
Open Our Eyes				2086		
Pass Me Not, O Gentle Savior	351		271			
People Need the Lord				2244		
Something Beautiful, Something Good	394		303			
Stay with Us				2199		115
There's a Wideness in God's Mercy	121					
Turn Your Eyes upon Jesus	349					
Victory in Jesus	370		92			
When Jesus the Healer Passed Through Galilee	263		171			
Wounded World that Cries for Healing				2177		

November 1, 2009 (All Saints)

Liturgical Color: White

Scripture Hymn Title	UMH	MVPC	CLUW	TFWS	SOZ	URW
Isaiah 25:6-9						
All Who Hunger				2126		
Arise, Shine Out, Your Light Has Come	725					
Canticle of Hope	734					
Canticle of the Turning						18
Christ Is Risen, Christ Is Living	313					
Christ Jesus Lay in Death's Strong Bands	319					
Christ the Victorious, Give to Your Servants	653		380			
Come to the Table				2264		
Come, We that Love the Lord (Marching to Zion)	733				3	13
Cristo Vive, Fuera el Llanto	313					
Eat This Bread, Drink This Cup	628					379
For All the Saints, Who from Their Labors Rest	711	384	388			
I Want to Be Ready	722				151	
O Day of Peace that Dimly Shines	729					
O Holy City, Seen of John	726		390			
O What Their Joy and Their Glory Must Be	727					
Rock of Ages, Cleft for Me	361	247				
Taste and See				2267		258
The Strife Is O'er, the Battle Done	306					
This Is a Day of New Beginnings	383	208	311			
We, Thy People, Praise Thee	67		72			
When All Is Ended						133
You Who Are Thirsty				2132		
Psalm 24						
All Glory, Laud, and Honor	280					
All People that on Earth Do Dwell	75		118			

Scripture Hymn Title	UMH	MVPC	CLUW	TFWS	SOZ	URW
Change My Heart, O God			278	2152		
Christ the Lord Is Risen				2116		
Come, Thou Almighty King	61	11				
For All the Saints, Who from Their Labors Rest	711	384	388			
Hail the Day that Sees Him Rise	312	158				
He Has Made Me Glad				2270		
Holy Ground				2272		
Honor and Praise				2018		
I Sing a Song of the Saints of God	712					
Let's Sing Unto the Lord (Cantemos al Señor)	149	49	67			
Lift Up Your Heads, Ye Mighty Gates	213					
Many and Great, O God, Are Thy Things	148	50	71			232
My Gratitude Now Accept, O Lord				2044		
Psalm 24 (King James Version)	212					
The King of Glory Comes				2091		
They Shall Receive a Blessing					209	
This Is My Father's World	144	47	62			71
Thou Art Worthy				2041		
What Gift Can We Bring	87					127

Revelation 21:1-6a

Scripture Hymn Title	UMH	MVPC	CLUW	TFWS	SOZ	URW
All Who Hunger				2126		
Arise, Shine Out, Your Light Has Come	725					
Awesome God				2040		
Beams of Heaven as I Go	524				10	
Blessed Quietness				2142	206	
Christ the Victorious, Give to Your Servants	653		380			
Come, Let Us Join Our Friends Above	709		387			
Come, We that Love the Lord (Marching to Zion)	733				3	139
Come, Ye Disconsolate, Where'er Ye Languish	510					
For All the Saints				2283		
For the Healing of the Nations	428					
From the Rising of the Sun				2024		
Glorious Things of Thee Are Spoken	731		256			
Here, O My Lord, I See Thee	623					

Scripture Hymn Title	UMH	MVPC	CLUW	TFWS	SOZ	URW
I Want to Be Ready	722				151	
I'll Fly Away				2282	183	
Joy Comes with the Dawn				2210		
Joy in the Morning				2284		
Love Divine, All Loves Excelling	384					100
My Faith Looks Up to Thee	452				215	
O Come and Dwell in Me	388					
O Day of Peace that Dimly Shines	729					
O Freedom				2194		
O God, Our Help in Ages Past	117					200
O Holy City, Seen of John	726		390			
O What Their Joy and Their Glory Must Be	727					
Open Our Eyes				2086		
Sing with All the Saints in Glory	702		382			
Soon and Very Soon	706		385		198	
Spirit Song	347	190	91			
There's a Spirit in the Air	192					
There's Something About that Name	171	74				
There's Within My Heart a Melody	380		289			
This Is a Day of New Beginnings	383	208	311			
This Is the Feast of Victory	638					
We Shall Overcome	533		140		127	
We Will Glorify the King of Kings				2087		
When All Is Ended						133
You Who Are Thirsty				2132		

John 11:32-44

Scripture Hymn Title	UMH	MVPC	CLUW	TFWS	SOZ	URW
All Hail the Power of Jesus' Name (CORONATION)	154	60				
All Hail the Power of Jesus' Name (DIADEM)	155					
Awake, O Sleeper, Rise from Death	551					
Christ the Victorious, Give to Your Servants	653		380			
How Blest Are They Who Trust in Christ	654					
How Firm a Foundation	529	256				
I Know Whom I Have Believed (I Know Not Why God's Wondrous Grace)	714		290			
I Sing a Song of the Saints of God	712					
In Thee Is Gladness	169					

Scripture Hymn Title	UMH	MVPC	CLUW	TFWS	SOZ	URW
O For a Thousand Tongues to Sing	57	1	226			
Rejoice, the Lord Is King (DARWALL'S 148TH)	715					
Rejoice, the Lord Is King (GOPSAL)	716					
Sing with All the Saints in Glory	702		382			
This Is a Day of New Beginnings	383	208	311			
When Jesus Wept				2106		
Why Has God Forsaken Me?				2110		

November 8, 2009 (Twenty-third Sunday after Pentecost)

Liturgical Color: Green

Scripture Hymn Title	UMH	MVPC	CLUW	TFWS	SOZ	URW
Ruth 3:1-5; 4:13-17						
As Man and Woman We Were Made	642					
Blessed Be the Name	63					
Blessed Be the Name of the Lord				2034		
Blest Be the Tie that Binds	557	347				
By Gracious Powers So Wonderfully Sheltered	517					
God of Many Names	105					
Lord, We Come to Ask Your Blessing				2230		
My Life Is in You, Lord				2032		
Praise the Lord Who Reigns Above	96	124				
The Care the Eagle Gives Her Young	118	302				199
The Family Prayer Song				2188		
When Love Is Found	643	343				
Your Love, O God, Has Called Us Here	647					
Psalm 127 or Psalm 42 (UMH 777)						
All Are Welcome						58
All I Need Is You				2080		
As the Deer			116	2025		267
Canticle of Love	646					
Creating God, Your Fingers Trace	109					
Forth in Thy Name, O Lord, I Go	438					
Happy the Home When God Is there	445					
The Care the Eagle Gives Her Young	118	302				199
The Family Prayer Song				2188		

Scripture Hymn Title	UMH	MVPC	CLUW	TFWS	SOZ	URW
Hebrews 9:24-28						
All Hail King Jesus				2069		
God of Many Names	105					
Hail, Thou Once Despised Jesus	325					
Hallelujah! What a Savior	165					
I'm So Glad Jesus Lifted Me				2151		
Jesus, Thine All-Victorious Love	422					
Living for Jesus				2149		
Love Divine, All Loves Excelling	384					100
Man of Sorrows! What a Name	165					
My God, I Love Thee	470					
Rejoice, the Lord Is King (DARWALL'S 148TH)	715					
Rejoice, the Lord Is King (GOPSAL)	716					
The Lily of the Valley				2062		
'Tis Finished! The Messiah Dies	282		182			
Victim Divine				2259		
Mark 12:38-44						
A Charge to Keep I Have	413					
All My Hope Is Firmly Grounded	132					
As Man and Woman We Were Made	642					
Bless Thou the Gifts	587		360			
Blest Are They				2155		163
Blest Be the Tie that Binds	557	347				
Give Thanks			247	2036		
I Want a Principle Within	410					
Jesu, Jesu, Fill Us with Your Love	432	288	179			116
Jesus, Thine All-Victorious Love	422					
Lord, Be Glorified				2150		
Lord, Whose Love Through Humble Service	581					204
More Precious than Silver				2065		
O Master, Let Me Walk with Thee	430		315			
O Young and Fearless Prophet	444					
Praise You				2003		
Take My Life, and Let It Be Consecrated	399		312			
The Gift of Love (Though I May Speak with Bravest Fire)	408		341			141

Scripture Hymn Title	UMH	MVPC	CLUW	TFWS	SOZ	URW
What Does the Lord Require	441					
What Gift Can We Bring	87					127
When the Poor Ones (Cuando El Pobre)	434	301	138			
Where Cross the Crowded Ways of Life	427	296				
Your Love, O God, Has Called Us Here	647					

November 15, 2009 (Twenty-fourth Sunday after Pentecost)

Liturgical Color: Green

Scripture Hymn Title	UMH	MVPC	CLUW	TFWS	SOZ	URW
1 Samuel 1:4-20						
A Mother Lined a Basket				2189		
Child of Blessing, Child of Promise	611		232			
Come, Ye Disconsolate, Where'er Ye Languish	510					
Give to the Winds Thy Fears	129		282			
Go Now in Peace	665		363			
I'll Praise My Maker While I've Breath	60		123			
If the World from You Withhold	522					
Kum Ba Yah, My Lord	494		332		139	
Leave It There	522				23	
My Soul Gives Glory to My God	198					
Not So in Haste, My Heart	455					
O God, Our Help in Ages Past	117					200
Rock of Ages, Cleft for Me	361	247				
Sweet Hour of Prayer	496	248	330			
Tell Out, My Soul, the Greatness of the Lord!	200					
The Care the Eagle Gives Her Young	118		302		199	
The Family Prayer Song				2188		
The Lord Bless and Keep You				2280		
When Our Confidence Is Shaken	505					
1 Samuel 2:1-10 or Psalm 113 (UMH 834)						
A Mighty Fortress Is Our God	110	25				271
Blest Are They				2155		163
Give Thanks			247	2036		
I'll Praise My Maker While I've Breath	60		123			

Scripture Hymn Title	UMH	MVPC	CLUW	TFWS	SOZ	URW
My Soul Gives Glory to My God	198					
O Worship the King, All-Glorious Above	73					
Praise to the Lord				2029		309
Praise to the Lord, the Almighty	139	29	68			63
Something Beautiful, Something Good	394		303			
Tell Out, My Soul, the Greatness of the Lord!	200					

Hebrews 10:11-14, (15-18), 19-25

Scripture Hymn Title	UMH	MVPC	CLUW	TFWS	SOZ	URW
Blessed Assurance, Jesus Is Mine!	369	65	287			
Blow Ye the Trumpet, Blow	379	309				
Come, Thou Fount of Every Blessing	400	42	127			92
Fix Me, Jesus	655				122	
I Am Thine, O Lord	419	218				
I Want to Be Ready	722				151	
Live in Charity (Ubi Caritas)				2179		394
Living for Jesus				2149		
Lord, Listen to Your Children				2207		
My Hope Is Built on Nothing Less	368	261				
My Lord, What a Morning	719		386		145	
Near to the Heart of God (There Is a Place of Quiet Rest)	472		324			
O For a Heart to Praise My God	417					
Since Jesus Came into My Heart				2140		
Steal Away to Jesus	704		378		134	
Swing Low, Sweet Chariot	703		384		104	
Take Our Bread	640		238			
There Are Some Things I May Not Know				2147		
There Is a Fountain Filled with Blood	622					
This Is the Feast of Victory	638					
'Tis Finished! The Messiah Dies	282		182			
Victim Divine				2259		
Wake, Awake, for Night Is Flying	720					
Wash, O God, Our Sons and Daughters	605					
When Our Confidence Is Shaken	505					

Scripture Hymn Title	UMH	MVPC	CLUW	TFWS	SOZ	URW

Mark 13:1-8

Scripture Hymn Title	UMH	MVPC	CLUW	TFWS	SOZ	URW
By Gracious Powers So Wonderfully Sheltered	517					
Canticle of the Turning						18
Fix Me, Jesus	655				122	
Freedom Is Coming				2192		
How Firm a Foundation	529	256				
I Know Whom I Have Believed (I Know Not Why God's Wondrous Grace)	714		290			
I Want to Be Ready	722					151
My Lord, What a Morning	719		386		145	
O Day of God, Draw Nigh	730					
O Freedom				2194		
Song of Hope				2186		
Soon and Very Soon	706		385		198	
Stand By Me	512				41	
Steal Away to Jesus	704		378		134	
Swing Low, Sweet Chariot	703		384		104	
Unsettled World				2183		
Wake, Awake, for Night Is Flying	720					
When the Storms of Life Are Raging	512					

November 22, 2009 (Christ the King/Reign of Christ)

Liturgical Color: White

Scripture Hymn Title	UMH	MVPC	CLUW	TFWS	SOZ	URW
2 Samuel 23:1-7						
God Is Here	660					
Hail to the Lord's Anointed	203	81				
I Will Call upon the Lord				2002		
Lo, He Comes with Clouds Descending	718					
O God Beyond All Praising				2009		
Praise the Name of Jesus				2066		
Righteous and Just Is the Word of Our Lord (La Palabra Del Señor Es Recta)	107					
Rock of Ages, Cleft for Me	361	247				
Surely the Presence of the Lord Is in This Place	328	344	215			
We Sing to You, O God				2001		293
What Does the Lord Require	441					
Psalm 132:1-12, (13-18)						
Bless the Lord				2013		377
God Is Here	660					
Jesus, We Want to Meet	661					
Jubilate, Servite				2017		383
O God, Our Help in Ages Past	117					200
O Lord, My Heart Is Not Proud (Psalm 131)						330
Surely the Presence of the Lord Is in This Place	328	344	215			
The Trees of the Field				2279		
Your Love, O God	120	26				

Scripture Hymn Title	UMH	MVPC	CLUW	TFWS	SOZ	URW

Revelation 1:4b-8

Scripture Hymn Title	UMH	MVPC	CLUW	TFWS	SOZ	URW
All Hail King Jesus				2069		
All Hail the Power of Jesus' Name (CORONATION)	154	60				
All Hail the Power of Jesus' Name (DIADEM)	155					
Awesome God				2040		
Blessed Assurance, Jesus Is Mine!	369	65	287			
Bring Forth the Kingdom				2190		
Christ Is Risen, Christ Is Living	313					
Come, Thou Almighty King	61	11				
Cristo Vive, Fuera el Llanto	313					
Freedom Is Coming				2192		
Glory Be to the Father (GREATOREX)	71					
Glory Be to the Father (MEINEKE)—Gloria Patri	70	23				
Hail to the Lord's Anointed	203	81				
He Is Exalted				2070		
Jesus Shall Reign Where'er the Sun	157					
King of Kings				2075		
Let All Mortal Flesh Keep Silence	626		150		217	
Lo, He Comes with Clouds Descending	718					
Love Divine, All Loves Excelling	384					100
Majesty, Worship His Majesty	176	171	204			
Maker, in Whom We Live	88					
My Tribute	99					
Of the Father's Love Begotten	184	52	66			
Rejoice, the Lord Is King (DARWALL'S 148TH)	715					
Rejoice, the Lord Is King (GOPSAL)	716					
Soon and Very Soon	706		385		198	
This Is the Feast of Victory	638					
Turn Your Eyes upon Jesus	349					
We Will Glorify the King of Kings				2087		
When Morning Gilds the Skies	185		369			184
Ye Watchers and Ye Holy Ones	90					
You Are Worthy				2063		

Scripture Hymn Title	UMH	MVPC	CLUW	TFWS	SOZ	URW

John 18:33-37

Scripture Hymn Title	UMH	MVPC	CLUW	TFWS	SOZ	URW
All Hail King Jesus				2069		
Awesome God				2040		
Hail, Thou Once Despised Jesus	325					
Hallelujah! What a Savior	165					
Here Am I				2178		
Let All Mortal Flesh Keep Silence	626	150		217		
Man of Sorrows! What a Name	165					
Morning Glory, Starlit Sky	194					
O Sing a Song of Bethlehem	179					
Rejoice, the Lord Is King (DARWALL'S 148TH)	715					
Rejoice, the Lord Is King (GOPSAL)	716					
Sent Out in Jesus' Name				2184		
We've a Story to Tell to the Nations	569					

November 26, 2009 (Thanksgiving Day—USA)

Liturgical Color: Red or White

Scripture Hymn Title	UMH	MVPC	CLUW	TFWS	SOZ	URW
Joel 2:21-27						
All Creatures of Our God and King	62	22				
Come, All of You	350					
Come, Ye Thankful People, Come	694		241			
Depth of Mercy! Can There Be	355		273			
Now Thank We All Our God	102					
Open Our Eyes				2086		
There's a Wideness in God's Mercy	121					
Una Espiga	637	319				
We Gather Together to Ask the Lord's Blessing	131	361				
We, Thy People, Praise Thee	67		72			
Psalm 126						
Bless His Holy Name				2015		
Come, Ye Disconsolate, Where'er Ye Languish	510					
Give to the Winds Thy Fears	129		282			
God Has Done Great Things for Us (Psalm 126)						326
Hail to the Lord's Anointed	203	81				
Joy Comes with the Dawn				2210		
Let's Sing Unto the Lord (Cantemos al Señor)	149	49	67			
O God, Our Help in Ages Past	117					200
O Spirit of the Living God	539					
Rejoice, Ye Pure in Heart (MARION)	160		130			
Rejoice, Ye Pure in Heart (VINEYARD HAVEN)	161					
The Trees of the Field				2279		

Scripture Hymn Title	UMH	MVPC	CLUW	TFWS	SOZ	URW
When God First Brought Us Back from Exile (Psalm 126)						325
When God Restored Our Common Life				2182		

1 Timothy 2:1-7

Scripture Hymn Title	UMH	MVPC	CLUW	TFWS	SOZ	URW
Christ Is the World's Light	188					
Come and Find the Quiet Center				2128		
Dona Nobis Pacem	376	360	142			443
Give Thanks			247	2036		
God of Many Names	105					
Jesus, Name above All Names				2071		
Let There Be Light	440					
Make Me a Channel of Your Peace				2171		
This Is My Song	437					
We Believe in One True God	85					

Matthew 6:25-33

Scripture Hymn Title	UMH	MVPC	CLUW	TFWS	SOZ	URW
All My Hope Is Firmly Grounded	132					
All Things Bright and Beautiful	147		63			
Be Still, My Soul	534		307			
Bring Forth the Kingdom				2190		
Cares Chorus				2215		
Children of the Heavenly Father	141		335			
For the Fruits of This Creation	97					193
Give Thanks			247	2036		
Give to the Winds Thy Fears	129		282			
God Be with You till We Meet Again (GOD BE WITH YOU)	672		347		37	
God Be with You till We Meet Again (RANDOLPH)	673					
God Is So Good				2056	231	
God Will Take Care of You (Nunca desmayes)	130	260				
Great Is Thy Faithfulness	140	30	81			
His Eye Is on the Sparrow				2146	33	
How Lovely, Lord, How Lovely				2042		
I Will Trust in the Lord	464		292		14	
If the World from You Withhold	522					
If Thou But Suffer God to Guide Thee	142					
Leave It There	522				23	

Scripture	Hymn Title	UMH	MVPC	CLUW	TFWS	SOZ	URW
	Praise Our God Above				2061		
	Rise to Greet the Sun	678		371			
	Seek Ye First the Kingdom of God	405	201	136			
	Someone Asked the Question				2144		
	You Satisfy the Hungry Heart	629					

December 2008

The General Board of Discipleship of The United Methodist Church, Center for Worship Recourcing; P.O. Box 340003, Nashville, TN 37203-0003.
Toll-free telephone: 877-899-2780, ext. 7070; Worship-Preaching-Music Web Site: http://www.umcworship.org; E-mail address: worshipcenter@gbod.org.

Sun	Mon	Tue	Wed	Thu	Fri	Sat
	1	2	3	4	5	6
7 2nd Sun of Advent Is 40:1-11; Ps 85:1-2, 8-13 (UMH 806); 2 Pet 3:8-15a; Mk 1:1-8	8	9	10	11	12	13
14 3rd Sun of Advent Is 61:1-4, 8-11; Ps 126 (UMH 847); 1 Thess 5:16-24; Jn 1:6-8, 19-28	15	16	17	18 Charles Wesley b.1707	19	20
21 4th Sun of Advent Winter Solstice 2 Sam 7:1-11, 16; Lk 1:47-55 (UMH 199); Rom 16:25-27; Lk 1:26-38	22	23	24 Christmas Eve Is 9:2-7; Ps 96 (UMH 815); Titus 2:11-14; Lk 2:1-20	25 Christmas Day Is 52:7-10; Ps 98 (UMH 818); Heb 1:1-4 (5-12); Jn 1:1-14	26 Kwanzaa Begins	27
28 1st Sunday after Christmas Day Is 61:10-62:3; Ps 148 (UMH 861); Gal 4:4-7; Lk 2:22-40	29	30	31 Watch Night Eccl 3:1-13; Ps 8 (UMH 743); Rev 21:1-6a; Mt 25:31-46			
Kwanzaa, Dec 26-Jan 1						

The General Board of Discipleship of The United Methodist Church, Center for Worship Recourcing; P.O. Box 340003; Nashville, TN 37203-0003.
Toll-free telephone: 877-899-2780, ext. 7070; Worship-Preaching-Music Web Site: http://www.umcworship.org.; E-mail address: worshipcenter@gbod.org.

Sun	Mon	Tue	Wed	Thu	Fri	Sat
Call to Prayer and Self-Denial (any period during January-March)	Week of Prayer for Christian Unity (Jan 18-25)			**1** New Year's Day Eccl 3:1-13; Ps 8 (UMH 743); Rev 21:1-6a; Mt 25:31-46	**2**	**3**
4 2nd Sun after Christmas (or Epiphany Sunday using Jan 6); Jer 31:7-14; Ps 147:12-20 (UMH 859); Eph 1:3-14; John 1:(1-9),10-18	**5** Twelfth Night	**6** Epiphany of the Lord (may be observed Jan 4) Is 60:1-6; Ps 72:1-7, 10-14 (UMH 795); Eph 3:1-12; Mt 2:1-12	**7**	**8**	**9**	**10**
11 Baptism of the Lord (1st Sun after Epiph) Gen 1:1-5; Ps 29 (UMH 761); Acts 19:1-7; Mk 1:4-11	**12**	**13** Korean American Day	**14**	**15**	**16**	**17**
18 2nd Sun after Epiph; Human Relations Day Ecumenical Sunday 1 Sam 3:1-10 (11-20); Ps 139:1-6, 13-18 (UMH 854); 1 Cor 6:12-20; Jn 1:43-51	**19** Martin Luther King, Jr. Day	**20**	**21**	**22**	**23**	**24**
25 3rd Sun after Epiph Jonah 3:1-5, 10; Ps 62:5-12 (UMH 787); 1 Cor 7:29-31; Mk 1:14-20	**26**	**27**	**28**	**29**	**30**	**31**

Yearly dates to be determined by the annual conference:
- Christian Education Sunday
- Rural Life Sunday
- Disability Awareness Sunday
- International Day of Prayer for the Persecuted Church

February 2009

The General Board of Discipleship of The United Methodist Church, Center for Worship Recurring; P.O. Box 340003, Nashville, TN 37203-0003.
Toll-free telephone: 877-899-2780, ext. 7070; Worship-Preaching-Music Web Site: http://www.umcworship.org; E-mail address: worshipcenter@gbod.org.

Sun	Mon	Tue	Wed	Thu	Fri	Sat
1 4th Sun after Epiph Deut 18:15-20; Ps 111 (UMH 832); 1 Cor 8:1-13; Mk 1:21-28	**2** Presentation of the Lord/ Candelmas; Groundhog Day; Mal 3:1-4; Ps 24 (UMH 755); Heb 2:14-18; Lk 2:22-40	**3**	**4**	**5**	**6**	**7**
8 5th Sun after Epiph Boy Scout Sun; Is 40:21-31; Ps 147:1-11, 20c (UMH 859); 1 Cor 9:16-23; Mk 1:29-39	**9**	**10**	**11**	**12** Lincoln's Birthday	**13**	**14** Valentine's Day
15 6th Sun after Epiph 2 Kings 5:1-14; Ps 30 (UMH 762); 1 Cor 9:24-27; Mk 1:40-45	**16** Presidents Day Washington's Birthday	**17**	**18**	**19**	**20**	**21**
22 Transfiguration Sun 2 Kings 2:1-12; Ps 50:1-6 (UMH 783); 2 Cor 4:3-6; Mk 9:2-9	**23**	**24** Shrove Tuesday	**25** Ash Wednesday Joel 2:1-2, 12-17; Ps 51:1-17 (UMH 785); 2 Cor 5:20b-6:10; Mt 6:1-6, 16-21	**26**	**27**	**28**
Feb: Black History Month	Brotherhood/Sister-hood Week: 3rd weeek of Feb					

2009

Sun	Mon	Tue	Wed	Thu	Fri	Sat
1 1st Sunday in Lent Gen 9:8-17; Ps 25:1-10 (UMH 756); 1 Pet 3:18-22; Mk 1:9-15	**2** John Wesley d. 1791	**3**	**4**	**5**	**6** World Day of Prayer	**7**
8 2nd Sunday in Lent Begins; Girl Scout Sun Gen 17:1-7, 15-16; Ps 22:23-31 (UMH 752); Rom 4:13-25, Mk 8:31-38	**9**	**10**	**11**	**12**	**13**	**14**
15 3rd Sun in Lent Ex 20:1-17; Ps 19 (UMH 750); 1 Cor 1:18-25; Jn 2:13-22	**16**	**17** St. Patrick's Day	**18**	**19**	**20**	**21**
22 4th Sunday in Lent; One Great Hour of Sharing; Num 21:4-9; Ps 107:1-3, 17-22 (UMH 830); Eph 2:1-10; Jn 3:14-21	**23**	**24**	**25**	**26**	**27**	**28**
29 5th Sunday in Lent Charles Wesley d. 1788 Jer 31:31-34; Ps 51:1-12 (UMH 785); Heb 5:5-10; Jn 12:20-33	**30**	**31**				

Daylight Saving Time

March: Women's History Month

The General Board of Discipleship of The United Methodist Church, Center for Worship Recource ing; P.O. Box 340003; Nashville, TN 37203-0003.
Toll-free telephone: 877-899-2780, ext. 7070; Worship-Preaching-Music Web Site: http://www.umcworship.org; E-mail address: worshipcenter@gbod.org

April — 2009

Sun	Mon	Tue	Wed	Thu	Fri	Sat
Religion in American Life Month: April			**1** April Fool's Day	**2**	**3**	**4**
5 Palm/Passion Sunday (see box below)	**6** Monday of Holy Week Is 42:1-9; Ps 36:5-11 (UMH 771); Heb 9:11-15; Jn 12:1-11	**7** Tuesday of Holy Week Is 49:1-7; Ps 71:1-14 (UMH 794); 1 Cor 1:18-31; Jn 12:20-36	**8** Wednesday of Holy Week Is 50:4-9a; Ps 70 (UMH 793); Heb 12:1-3; Jn 13:21-32	**9** Holy Thursday Ex 12:1-4 (5-10), 11-14; Ps 116:1-2, 12-19; (UMH 837); 1 Cor 11:23-26; Jn 13:1-17, 31b-35	**10** Good Friday Is 52:13-53:12; Ps 22 (UMH 752); Heb 10:16-25; Jn 18:1-19:42	**11** Easter Vigil (see box below)
12 Easter Day Acts 10:34-43; Ps 118:1-2, 14-24 (UMH 839); 1 Cor 15:1-11; Jn 20:1-18 (or Mk 16:1-8)	**13**	**14**	**15** USA Federal Income Tax Due	**16** Holocaust Memorial Day	**17**	**18**
19 2nd Sun of Easter Acts 4:32-35; Ps 133 (UMH 850); 1 Jn 1:1-2:2; John 20:19-31	**20**	**21**	**22** Earth Day Administrative Assistants' Day	**23**	**24** Arbor Day	**25**
26 3rd Sun of Easter; Native American Ministries Sunday; Acts 3:12-19; Ps 4 (UMH 741); 1 Jn 3:1-7; Lk 24:36b-48	**27**	**28**	**29**	**30**		

PALM/PASSION SUNDAY: Liturgy of the Palms: Mk 11:1-11; Ps 118:1-2, 19-29 (UMH 839); Liturgy of the Passion: Is 50:4-9a; Ps 31:9-16 (UMH 764); Phil 2:5-11; Mk 14:1-15:47 or Mk 15:1-39, (40-47)

EASTER VIGIL: The number of readings may vary, but Exodus 14 and at least two other readings from the Old Testament should be used in addition to the New Testament readings. Old Testament Readings and Psalms: Gen 1:1-2:4a; Is 55:1-11; Ps 136:1-9, 23-26, or Ps 33 (UMH 767); Is 12:2-6; Gen 7:1-5, 11-18; 8:6-18; 9:8-13; Ezek 36:24-28; Ps 42 (UMH 777); Ps 46 (UMH 780); Gen 22:1-18; Ezek 37:1-14; Ps 16 (UMH 748); Ex 14:10-31; 15:20-21; Ex 15:1b-13, 17-18 (UMH 135); Second Reading and Ps: Rom 6:3-11; Ps 114 (UMH 835); Gospel Reading: Mk 16:1-8

The General Board of Discipleship of The United Methodist Church, Center for Worship Resourcing; P.O. Box 340003, Nashville, TN 37203-0003. Toll-free telephone: 877-899-2780, ext. 7070; Worship-Preaching-Music Web Site: http://www.umcworship.org; E-mail address: worshipcenter@gbod.org.

Sun	Mon	Tue	Wed	Thu	Fri	Sat
May: Asian Pacific American Heritage Month; Christian Home Month; National Family Week (May 4-10)	May 24: Aldersgate Day and Heritage Sunday				**1** May Fellowship Day	**2**
3 4th Sun of Easter Golden Cross Sunday Acts 4:5-12; Ps 23 (UMH 754 or 137); 1 Jn 3:16-24; Jn 10:11-18	**4**	**5** Cinco de Mayo	**6**	**7** National Day of Prayer	**8**	**9**
10 5th Sun of Easter; Mothers Day; Festival of the Christian Home; Acts 8:26-40; Ps 22:25-31 (UMH 752); 1 Jn 4:7-21; Jn 15:1-8	**11**	**12**	**13**	**14**	**15**	**16** Armed Forces Day
17 6th Sun of Easter Acts 10:44-48; Ps 98 (UMH 818); 1 Jn 5:1-6; Jn 15:9-17	**18**	**19**	**20**	**21** Ascension of the Lord (may be used May 24) Acts 1:1-11; Ps 47 (UMH 781); Eph 1:15-23; Lk 24:44-53	**22**	**23**
24 7th Sun of Easter (or Ascension Sunday) Acts 1:15-17, 21-26; Ps 1 (UMH 738); 1 Jn 5:9-13; Jn 17:6-19	**25** Memorial Day	**26**	**27**	**28**	**29**	**30**
31 Day of Pentecost Acts 2:1-21; Ps 104:24-34, 35b (UMH 826); Rom 8:22-27; Jn 15:26-27; 16:4b-15						

June 2009

The General Board of Discipleship of The United Methodist Church, Center for Worship Recourcing; P.O. Box 340003; Nashville, TN 37203-0003.
Toll-free telephone: 877-899-2780, ext. 7070; Worship-Preaching-Music Web Site: http://www.umcworship.org; E-mail address: worshipcenter@gbod.org.

Sun	Mon	Tue	Wed	Thu	Fri	Sat
	1	2	3	4	5	6
7 Trinity Sun (1st Sun after Pentecost); Peace with Justice Sun; Is 6:1-8; Ps 29 (UMH 761); Rom 8:12-17; Jn 3:1-17	8	9	10	11	12	13
14 Flag Day 1 Sam 15:34-16:13; Ps 20 or Ps 92 (UMH 811); 2 Cor 5:6-10 (11-13), 14-17; Mk 4:26-34	15	16	**17** John Wesley b. 1703	18	**19** Juneteenth	20
21 Fathers Day; 1 Sam 17: (1a, 4-11, 19-23), 32-49; Ps 9:9-20 (UMH 744); 2 Cor 6:1-13; Mk 4:35-41	22	23	24	25	26	27
28 2 Sam 1:1, 17-27; Ps 130 (UMH 848); 2 Cor 8:7-15; Mk 5:21-43	29	30				

The General Board of Discipleship of The United Methodist Church, Center for Worship Recourcing; P.O. Box 340003; Nashville, TN 37203-0003. Toll-free telephone: 877-899-2780, ext. 7070; Worship-Preaching-Music Web Site: http://www.umcworship.org.; E-mail address: worshipcenter@gbod.org.

July 2009

Sun	Mon	Tue	Wed	Thu	Fri	Sat
			1	2	3	4 USA Independence Day Deut 10:12-13, 17-21; Ps 72 (UMH 795); Gal 5:13-26; Jn 8:31-39
5 2 Sam 5:1-5, 9-10; Ps 48 (UMH 782); 2 Cor 12:2-10; Mk 6:1-13	6	7	8	9	10	11
12 2 Sam 6:1-5, 12b-19; Ps 24 (UMH 755); Eph 1:3-14; Mk 6:14-29	13	14	15	16	17	18
19 2 Sam 7:1-14a; Ps 89:20-37 (UMH 807); Eph 2:11-22; Mk 6:30-34, 53-56	20	21	22	23	24	25
26 Great Day of Singing; Parents Day; 2 Sam 11:1-15; Ps 14 (UMH 746); Eph 3:14-21; Jn 6:1-21	27	28	29	30	31	

August 2009

The General Board of Discipleship of The United Methodist Church, Center for Worship Recourcing; P.O. Box 340003; Nashville, TN 37203-0003.
Toll-free telephone: 877-899-2780, ext. 7070; Worship-Preaching-Music Web Site: http://www.umcworship.org; E-mail address: worshipcenter@gbod.org.

Sun	Mon	Tue	Wed	Thu	Fri	Sat
A Great Day of Singing (any Sunday during the year, or August)						1
2 2 Sam 11:26-12:13a; Ps 51:1-12 (UMH 785); Eph 4:1-16; Jn 6:24-35	3	4	5	6	7	8
9 2 Sam 18:5-9, 15, 31-33; Ps 130 (UMH 848); Eph 4:25-5:2; Jn 6:35, 41-51	10	11	12	13	14	15
16 1 Kgs 2:10-12; 3:3-14; Ps 111 (UMH 832); Eph 5:15-20; Jn 6:51-58	17	18	19	20	21	22
23 1 Kgs 8:(1, 6, 10-11), 22-30, 41-43; Ps 84 (UMH 804); Eph 6:10-20; Jn 6:56-69	24	25	26	27	28	29
30 Song 2:8-13; Ps 45:1-2, 6-9 or Ps 72 (UMH 795); Jas 1:17-27; Mk 7:1-8, 14-15, 21-23	31					

September

The General Board of Discipleship of The United Methodist Church, Center for Worship Resourcing; P.O. Box 340003; Nashville, TN 37203-0003.
Toll-free telephone: 877-899-2780, ext. 7070; Worship-Preaching-Music Web Site: http://www.umcworship.org; E-mail address: worshipcenter@gbod.org.

2009

Sun	Mon	Tue	Wed	Thu	Fri	Sat
Hispanic Heritage Month: Sep 15 – Oct 15		1	2	3	4	5
6 Grandparents Day Prov 22:1-2, 8-9, 22-23; Ps 125 or Ps 124 (UMH 846); Jas 2:1-10, (11-13, 14-17; Mk 7:24-37	**7** Labor Day	8	9	10	**11** Patriot Day	12
13 Prov 1:20-33; Ps 19 (UMH 750); Jas 3:1-12; Mk 8:27-38	**14** Columbus Day	15	16	**17** Citizenship Day	18	19
20 Prov 31:10-31; Ps 1 (UMH 738); Jas 3:13-4:3, 7-8a; Mk 9:30-37	21	22	23	24	25	26
27 Esth 7:1-6, 9-10; 9:20-22; Ps 124 (UMH 846); Jas 5:13-20; Mk 9:38-50	28	29	30	31		

October 2009

The General Board of Discipleship of The United Methodist Church, Center for Worship Recources; P.O. Box 340003; Nashville, TN 37203-0003. Toll-free telephone: 877-899-2780, ext. 7070; Worship-Preaching-Music Web Site: http://www.umcworship.org; E-mail address: worshipcenter@gbod.org.

Sun	Mon	Tue	Wed	Thu	Fri	Sat
Hispanic Heritage Month: Sep 15 – Oct 15			1	Thu	**2**	**3**
4 World Communion Job 1:1; 2:1-10; Ps 26 or Ps 25 (UMH 756); Heb 1:1-4; 2:5-12; Mk 10:2-16	**5**	**6**	**7**	**8**	**9** Children's Sabbath (Oct 9-11)	**10**
11 Job 23:1-9, 16-17; Ps 22:1-15 (UMH 752); Heb 4:12-16; Mk 10:17-31	**12** Canadian Thanksgiving Day Joel 2:21-27; Ps 126 (UMH 847); 1 Tim 2:1-7; Mt 6:25-33	**13**	**14**	**15**	**16**	**17**
18 Laity Sunday Job 38:1-7, (34-41); Ps 104:1-9, 24, 35c (UMH 826); Heb 5:1-10; Mk 10:35-45	**19**	**20**	**21**	**22**	**23**	**24** United Nations Day
25 Job 42:1-6, 10-17; Ps 34:1-8, (19-22) (UMH 769); Heb 7:23-28; Mk 10:46-52	**26**	**27**	**28**	**29**	**30**	**31** Reformation Day; Halloween

November 2009

The General Board of Discipleship of The United Methodist Church, Center for Worship Recourcing; P.O. Box 340003; Nashville, TN 37203-0003.
Toll-free telephone: 877-899-2780, ext. 7070; Worship-Preaching-Music Web Site: http://www.umcworship.org; E-mail address: worshipcenter@gbod.org.

Sun	Mon	Tue	Wed	Thu	Fri	Sat
1 All Saints' Day Daylight Saving Time Ends; Is 25:6-9; Ps 24 (UMH 755); Rev 21:1-6a; Jn 11:32-44	**2**	**3** USA Election Day	**4**	**5**	**6**	**7**
8 Organ and Tissue Donor Sun; Ruth 3:1-5; 4:13-17; Ps 127 or Ps 42 (UMH 777); Heb 9:24-28; Mk 12:38-44	**9**	**10**	**11** Veterans Day	**12**	**13**	**14**
15 Bible Sunday; 1 Sam 1:4-20; 1 Sam 2:1-10 or Ps 113 (UMH 834); Heb 10:11-14 (15-18), 19-25; Mk 13:1-8	**16**	**17**	**18**	**19**	**20**	**21**
22 Christ the King/Reign of Christ; 2 Sam 23:1-7; Ps 132:1-12 (13-18) (UMH 849); Rev 1:4b-8; Jn 18:33-37	**23**	**24**	**25**	**26** USA Thanksgiving Day Joel 2:21-27; Ps 126 (UMH 847); 1 Tim 2:1-7; Mt 6:25-33	**27**	**28**
29 1st Sun of Advent; UM Student Day; Jer 33:14-16; Ps 25:1-10 (UMH 756); 1 Thess 3:9-13; Lk 21:25-36	**30**	**31**				

National Bible Week
(Nov 15-22)